IMAGES
of America

McHenry County

ILLINOIS

IMAGES
of America

McHenry County

ILLINOIS

Maryan and Dan Pelland

ARCADIA
PUBLISHING

Published by Arcadia Publishing
Charleston, South Carolina

Library of Congress Catalog Card Number: 2001088706

For all general information contact Arcadia Publishing at:
Telephone 843-853-2070
Fax 843-853-0044
E-mail sales@arcadiapublishing.com
For customer service and orders:
Toll-Free 1-888-313-2665

Visit us on the Internet at www.arcadiapublishing.com

A COMMUNITY OF FARMS, FAMILIES, AND PROGRESS. This farm, located on Barreville Road in McHenry, is typical of how land has been used for nearly 200 years. Times have changed and the roar of progress is heard across the country. Like many large farms, this one was divided into smaller parcels and parts of it were sold off. Land has been redivided or subdivided often to accommodate phenomenal growth. (Courtesy McHenry County Historical Society.)

CONTENTS

FRUIT OF THE LAND. Local fall crops include pumpkins, squash, corn, and gourds, and field fresh fruits and vegetables, almost taken for granted by local shoppers. This farm is on Crystal Lake Blacktop, McHenry. Most folks still tell you to "take the blacktop out of Crystal Lake and go north," though the dirt roads are long gone and the paved version is officially Crystal Lake Road. (Photo by Dan Pelland.)

ACKNOWLEDGMENTS

In 1963, Dorothy W. McEachren cared enough to found the McHenry County Historical Society—our communities are indebted to her for the riches contained in the drawers, files, bins, nooks, and crannies at the Society library and the museum in Union, Illinois. We could not have compiled this book but for the volunteers who maintain the collection now under the dedicated direction of Nancy Fike—thank you. The images in this volume, unless otherwise noted, are from the Society's collection and used with their kind permission.

Thanks to Mr. Don Peasley, whose intuitive eye and boundless energy gave our county a priceless photographic record of people and events from 1950 to the present. Thanks to Mr. Jim Keefe and family for generously walking us through their collection and lending wonderful images, notes, and personal remembrances. We appreciate Margaret and Henry Szlachta's time and materials. Thanks also to Hughes Hybrid Seeds, Inc. and the Hughes family for putting history at our disposal. Our gratitude also goes to Diana Kenny and the Crystal Lake Historical Society for graciously opening the Dole Mansion and the Society's resources to us. A special thanks to the reference department at the Woodstock Library for always being there. We would have been lost without the Marengo, Harvard, Cary, Algonquin and McHenry Libraries. Lastly, we thank the families and businesses that had the foresight and clear-headedness to preserve history and the willingness to share it with the public.

INTRODUCTION

McHenry County, Illinois, is a picture perfect farming community in the Heartland of Midwestern America. For nearly two centuries, a portion of the nation's food supply has come from this fertile land near the Fox River. The area played a key role in the history of Chicago and the United States from earliest days to the 21st century. But if you live here or visit here, the interesting thing is, you get no sense of aggrandizement, pomp, or inflated egos. People go about their business, raise their families, do their work, and make their contributions to society because that's what they want to do.

It's been said that all of the world's events and each of her people are only removed from each other by a tiny degree of separation. The history of our county is a clear demonstration of that theory. The American version of the silo was invented here, an indispensable contribution to farming. Stephen A. Douglas thought this county so pivotal that he made a special trip to woo voters here during his political battles. Jane Addams implored audiences at our opera houses to help her establish Hull House. Count Leo Tolstoy came here.

World-renowned hymns were penned here. Lincoln's Secretary of State William Seward had family here, as did President Gerald Ford, whose mother was a resident. Paul V. Galvin, founder of Motorola, spent his formative years here—earning his first income by selling refreshments to travelers at the Harvard train station. Frank Howard, who perfected a metal casting technique that helped win World War II, lived here. Dozens of Hollywood greats, including Paul Newman and Orson Wells, came from our opera houses. The list is long and fascinating. Beneath the placid scenery and quiet family communities, there have always been people boiling with a spirit of endeavor, a desire to succeed and the support network to make it happen.

The images you'll see here represent the period from the mid-1800s to the second half of the 20th century. It is unlikely that any other century in the history of the world brought as many changes to people's lives as this period did. We tried to put McHenry County's story in context with the rest of the country and the world during that time. It was our goal to show life here against a backdrop of international wars, national social struggles, and technological advances in an expanding world. We encourage you to imagine how your parents, grandparents, or even great grandparents must have felt as stagecoaches gave rise to trains, then automobiles, airplanes, jets, space travel, and finally, cyberspace. It is not unlikely that many people's lives have encompassed most or all of that kaleidoscope of innovation.

In the early days of this community, life was centralized. It was a good day's work to take care of yourself, your family, and perhaps some land. By the time the last photograph was made, our lives would encompass local, national, international, and universal issues. Perhaps the only way to encourage healthy growth in the present is to keep an eye on your roots. The past has a lot to teach us. We agree with Arcadia Publishing that we all have an obligation to preserve and share the story of how we got here.

We decided to compile this book because we raised our family here and are very pleased with how that project turned out. At least in part, we credit our community for the quality of life we enjoy here and wanted to share a panorama of that lifestyle. We are not historians, Dan and I. This book is not intended to be a diligent chronology or a perfectly organized complete history of the area. That's all been done before, and thoroughly. It was never our intent to parade the political icons of the past or present across our pages, though we acknowledge their relevance to the past and present. We simply set out to paint a picture of what life looked and felt like from the early days to the new millennium. From log cabins to concrete and steel, it's a fascinating story.

It's been a wonderful adventure, putting this book together. It reinforced, for us, the notion that the film camera was truly one of the most significant inventions of the last 200 years, and cemented our own love affair with the magic of image making. McHenry County photographers captured for you the record of how our neighbors, past and present, lived—you'll witness bright successes and perhaps some sad but edifying failures along the way. A widely divergent group of everyday people took up their view cameras, Brownies, Instamatics, or 35mms, and preserved, on ordinary paper coated with silver and gelatin, the way things were. Perhaps you can do the same for the next generation.

One

THE 19TH CENTURY

The sky's deep blue could make your heart ache. Virgin forests and prairies full of wild flowers, herbs, and medicines claimed the Illinois land. The Fox River tumbled, releasing the pungent smell of clean water, fish, and wetland plants into unpolluted air. That's what the earliest settlers of European descent found when they came to McHenry County in the 1830s when all of America was growing west. Ethnic settlements grew up: Dutch, Swedish, German, Irish, Scottish, Hispanic, and others. Our street and town names reflect this heritage. They came in wagons, by stagecoach, on horseback, and even on foot—adventurous individuals, families looking for a new way of life, entrepreneurs. They dug in, cleared and turned the land, built their homes and started their businesses. Back then, you really could be anything you wanted, if you were willing to struggle, think, and accomplish. Creature comforts were scarce for some. Family fortunes made life easier for others; and hard work was the great equalizer. Some of those families are still here, joined by others to farm, build industries, open stores, and raise families away from crowded cities. Once you get to know how it was for these folks, you won't wonder why they stayed.

WOODSTOCK FIRE DEPARTMENT, C.1890s. These men contended with frequent fires, arson, and accidents. They are outside the opera house, which was also the firehouse from 1895 until after the middle of the 20th century. Did the wooden ramps and sidewalks contribute to the frequent fires? (Courtesy the James Keefe Photo Collection.)

INCREDIBLY INTERESTING PHOTO, C. 1900. Mr. and Mrs. Jack Ford's cabin (they are on the bench, left) on the occasion of a neighborhood picnic. There weren't many black families, but most were treated with dignity, according to early remembrances. The menu here included: pickles, corn, white cake, bread, sandwiches, coffee, meats, and brown bread. The guests were Mrs. Charles Strickland, Mrs. J.T. Beldin, Mrs. Frank Loomis, Mrs. D. Morris, Mrs. William

Casely, Mrs. Moses Dimon, Mrs. Daniel Boyington, Mrs. M.E. Bushaw, and Mrs. Samuel Rowlands. The cabin was at the corner of Dietz and Forest Streets in Marengo. This is a beautiful example of early photography. The calf and dog are looking straight into the camera as if they've never seen anything like it. These folk may have never had their picture taken, either. (Courtesy Marengo Public Library.)

INVENTING THE SILO. In 1869, Fred Hatch studied agriculture at Illinois Industrial University (now University of Illinois). Fred, credited by *Dairymen Magazine* with inventing the vertical silo, cajoled his father into trying it. Lewis reluctantly agreed to build an eight-foot deep rock and mortar container inside his Spring Grove barn, extending 16 feet above. They raised the fattest, most productive cows around and gleefully built two more silos. (Courtesy the McHenry County Historical Society.)

TYPICAL BARN, FROM THE DOLE PROPERTY. This photo was made in 1885 in Crystal Lake, an excellent representation of that time, and interestingly, not much different from today's barns. Old barns decay and fall; this particular one is long gone. Suburban homeowners salvage barn board for paneling; beams are recycled into home building projects. (Courtesy Crystal Lake Historical Society.)

THE DOCTOR IS IN, SOUTHEAST CORNER STATE AND WASHINGTON. Here you can see the First National Bank in Marengo at the turn of the last century. Look closely at the top window (center front): the dentist who rented space from the bank looks ominously like someone waiting for a victim. His leather apron may tell you how much precision and care was used in dentistry. (Courtesy Marengo Public Library.)

EARLY COMMERCIAL VENTURES. State Street, Marengo, looking south. This prairie town bustled with meatpacking houses, a farm implement manufacturer, a railroad repair shop, and a flour mill. The clop of horses' feet gave way to the putt-putt of early autos and the roar of modern traffic. (Courtesy Marengo Public Library.)

A GRACIOUS OLD VICTORIAN LADY. This grand painted lady was built for Mr. C.P. Barnes who moved to Woodstock in about 1891, at age 19. The home, which stands on Madison Street and was featured as the rooming house in "Groundhog Day," cost $10,000 to build. This is how it looks today. It's very typical of upper middle class Victorian architecture, much showier than house kits mail-ordered from Sears. (Photo by Dan Pelland.)

DINING ROOM, C. 1883. There are few opportunities to explore contemporary Victorian room settings. This photo was done toward the end of the 19th century. The hand carved woodwork and room size carpets are symbols of wealth and station. The bow and powder horns seem odd in a formal setting, but were fairly common accouterments. Over the sideboard are stuffed birds, maybe peahens. (Courtesy Crystal Lake Historical Society.)

VICTORIAN OSTENTATIOUS DÉCOR. This china cabinet is typically Victorian. Ornate woodcarving showed the owner's wealth. Well-to-do Victorians displayed practically everything they owned. The more bric-a-brac, glassware, and gewgaws you had, the more affluent you were—especially if you hired people to dust it all. The Chinese theme was common—in rosewood, mahogany, walnut, or other highly polished hardwood. (Courtesy the Crystal Lake Historical Society.)

DOLE MANSION PARLOR INTERIOR. Victorian homes were more packed with international artifacts than museums were. Jars and urns were popular, especially from India, Africa, and the Orient. Huge mirrors reflected light in dark interiors, but they also related to spiritualistic beliefs—mirrors ward off negative energy. This exquisite mantle and mirror were lost as the mansion changed hands, but the restoration committee acquired a pair very like the originals. (Courtesy the Crystal Lake Historical Society.)

WEST VIEW, THE DOLE MANSION, CRYSTAL LAKE. Chicago businessman Charles S. Dole built his home in the 1860s on 1,000 acres of land bordering the lake. It cost $100,000. European craftsmen used black walnut trees from the property to create lavishly carved woodwork, parquet floors, and archways. Marble fireplaces graced several rooms. The Lakeside Center addition is now off the south side of the home. Mr. Dole was ostentatious and used to having his own way. When he wanted cows, they were imported from Scotland; when he grew interested in racehorses, he built a racecourse on the property and the finest horses were imported; when his daughter married, the wedding was like none ever seen in the area. The Doles moved on in the late 1890s and the property was owned by a series of ice companies before it was sold to Mrs. Lou Ringling. (Courtesy Crystal Lake Historical Society.)

THEN AND NOW, VIEWS OF CRYSTAL LAKE. This is the same view as the photo on page 21, taken across the lawn of the Dole Mansion. This image was made in December 2000 with the photographer standing at the same vantage point as the original shot, on the northwest side porch. Some of the oaks surrounding the circular drive of the property may have been planted during the Dole's tenure. The lawns are still well maintained, but the property is considerably smaller than Mr. Dole would have liked. The lakeshore has changed dramatically with the addition of a public beach, park district buildings, and a playground. (Photo by Dan Pelland.)

DANIEL FROHMAN Presents
AMERICA'S FOREMOST FILM ACTRESS,

MARY PICKFORD

IN THE FAMOUS TALE
OF A WOMAN'S
UNCONQUERABLE FAITH,

"TESS OF THE STORM COUNTRY"

By
GRACE·MILLER WHITE,
PRODUCED BY THE
FAMOUS PLAYERS FILM CO.
ADOLPH ZUKOR, PRES.

"THEY HEV TOOKEN EVERYTHING
AWAY FROM ME BUT GOD."

MARENGO ILL

OPERA HOUSE
FRIDAY NIGH
lo & 15 ct

MARY PICKFORD, AMERICA'S SWEETHEART. Melodrama was all the rage. Moviegoers lined up at the Marengo Opera House, El Tovar in Crystal Lake (currently the site of a multi-million dollar renovation project), the Princess in Woodstock and other venues to weep at the plight of poor Tess. For 15¢, you could find out why the diminutive Hollywood starlet's character wails pitifully, "They hev tooken everything from me but God." Interesting note: The night El Tovar opened for the first time, someone tossed a stink bomb in and cleared the auditorium. (Courtesy the McHenry County Historical Society.)

WEST FACADE. DOLE MANSION, 1883. This photo is shot from northwest of the house. The canvas tarp on the right end is actually a roll-up awning to keep the setting sun from overheating the house in summer. Mr. Dole had a tower room on the roof, reached by a 24-inch wide staircase. He was overseer of his world from that vantage point. (Courtesy Crystal Lake Historical Society.)

TOP BRASS. Life was simple, community was important, and most everyone participated in one way or another. Sing-alongs, sleigh rides, hayrides, and concerts in the park were typical Sunday diversions. This group of young men was part of the Woodstock City band—they played all over the area, but looked especially good on the city square. The only person identified is Merritt Thomas, second row, center. (Courtesy the McHenry County Historical Society.)

DOLE FAMILY WEDDING TENT. The lavish wedding party for the Dole's daughter accommodated hundreds of guests. This was the caterer's tent where dinner was laid out buffet style. Imagine how uncomfortable these guests had to be in layers of finery and sweltering in summer heat. But, as they said, "Let us be elegant or die!" (Courtesy Crystal Lake Historical Society.)

A COVERED WALKWAY FOR VIPS. This is a the canvas-covered path from the C&NW Railroad drop-off point on Charles Dole's property. The tunnel shaded wedding guests (the temperature was well above 80 degrees that wedding day in 1883). It terminated at the front door. Revelers carried on all day and the party was talked about all over the county for months afterward. Note that this outdoor walkway was carpeted. (Courtesy Crystal Lake Historical Society.)

CRYSTAL LAKE ACROSS DOLE MANSION LAWN. When ice companies finished with the mansion, it lay empty for years until the Lake Development Company bought it. Mrs. Al "Lou" Ringling, a snake charmer, was vice president—her picture hangs in the dining room now. The company built a huge addition (Lakeside Center) and the property became the first country club in the area. See a modern view on page 17. (Courtesy Crystal Lake Historical Society.)

LONG SUMMERS MEANT COUNTRY VISITS. This is Camp Epworth, Garden Prairie. Pictured, from left to right, are: (front row) unknown, unknown, Mrs. Dr. Adams, Mrs. William Woodard, unknown, unknown, Mrs. Smith Rogers, Mrs. Thayer; (second row) unknown, unknown, Mrs. Cohoun, Miss Grace Steard, unknown, unknown; (back row) Sylvia Standish, Mrs. Charles Robb, Mrs. Lester Barber, Miss Lucy Barrett, unknown, Arliss (?), unknown, Frances Sears, and Mrs. Horace Barber. (Courtesy the McHenry County Historical Society.)

21

Lotus Flower & Buds, Grass Lake, Ill. 67

LOTUS BEDS AT GRASS LAKE. A gentle time—white tulle skirts, parasols, and quiet boat excursions characterized Sunday afternoons. One destination was the lotus beds at Grass Lake. Excursion companies carried passengers to the expanse of white blooms, and photographer C. Childs caught it with his camera around the turn of the 19th century. Imagine soft guitar chords or lilting ukulele notes as the boat skimmed the water. (Courtesy the McHenry County Historical Society.)

GOING UP RIVER ON A SUNDAY AFTERNOON. What could be more idyllic? Soft breezes rustling the trees along the banks of the Fox. A dozen to twenty people per boat—ladies in pastel gowns, gentlemen in suits and bowlers. Pretty summer cottages and showy mansions visible along the shores. The boats traveled up river to the lotus beds and back for a few pennies fare. (Courtesy the McHenry County Historical Society.)

WOODSTOCK OPERA HOUSE, A GEM. This has been a crown jewel of Woodstock since its construction as city offices, police department, library, and fire department in 1890. "Steamboat Gothic" architecture became the perfect setting for musical evenings. The interior was restored in the 1970s. The Opera House was featured in the film *Groundhog Day*. Its audiences have seen live performances by Orson Wells, Geraldine Page, and Paul Newman. (Courtesy the McHenry County Historical Society.)

THE PRINCESS THEATER. A wonderful early photo of the Princess Theater, Woodstock, now the Woodstock Movie Theater. You can see the organ in front of the stage—Charles Clemming played the organ for silent film at the theater, and doubled as the organist at the funeral home for many years. The Princess Theater was later the Miller Theater. (Courtesy the James Keefe collection.)

THE VILLAGE SMITHY. Life wasn't all pretty scenery and leisure time. Horses needed shoes, farmers needed tools, tools needed repairs. This shop was typical around the turn of the 20th century. Smith shops lasted well into the century—filled with tools, scrap iron, and the indigenous sound of the hammer clanging on iron at the forge. The skill was passed generation to generation. Charles Gumprecht is second from the left. (Courtesy the McHenry County Historical Society.)

BOAT BUILDING THEN AND NOW. In 1888 the Hunter Weckler boat company was established in the Village of McHenry. They created custom boats for industry and personal use and ran excursion boats to the lotus beds via Fox River. A fire in 1916 destroyed 148 boats; another in 1930 did $25,000 damage and took 21 boats. Even against this adversity, the boat maker is one of several that survived to recent times. (Courtesy the McHenry County Historical Society.)

MOUNTING DEPARTMENT—OLIVER TYPEWRITER COMPANY, LYNN SHERM, FOREMAN. Rev. Thomas Oliver of the Methodist Episcopal Church developed the Oliver typewriter. He had a vision one night in 1886, wrote it down, and worked on the idea until he revolutionized "primitive writing machines." The reverend's plant, near the railroad station, employed 1,400 people. It closed in 1928. Rev. Oliver was, coincidentally, born in Woodstock, Ontario, Canada. (Courtesy the McHenry County Historical Society.)

FARMING AND BUSINESS. Farms, the lifeblood of the county, expanded. Businesses like International Harvester dispatched sales representatives out to the farmers. These are representative William Stoffel's customers—each purchased a spreader. He treated them to dinner at Riverside House, and then they hitched up their spreaders and paraded through town. Stoffel is second from right, first row. (Courtesy the McHenry County Historical Society.)

BE SURE AND MEET ME AT THE
GREAT McHENRY COUNTY FAIR,
At WOODSTOCK, ILLS., Sept. 11, 12, 13 and 14, 1888.
I SHALL BE THERE   P. S.—SEND FOR LIST.
A. S. WRIGHT, Secretary.

McHENRY COUNTY FAIR ADVERTISING CARDS, 1888. McHenry County devised its legendary county fair about this time. These are good examples of early advertising collectables, all the rage then and now. Some ad cards sell currently for thousands of dollars; many were created locally and represented events like the Fair and garnered thousands of attendees. Now the Fair is advertised on television, radio, and newspapers. (Courtesy the Henry and Margaret Szlachta Collection.)

RAILROAD RIGHT OF WAY CALCULATOR. On the edge of a new century the railroads rushed to grab land. This is the first page of a list that calculated the railroad right-of-way for the Cook, Lake, and McHenry County access across privately owned land (note Lewis Hatch's farm). Those rights-of-way have been continuous to the present day. Now hundreds of thousand of commuters travel the same routes each month. (Courtesy the McHenry County Historical Society.)

Two

FROM 1900 TO 1909

This was a time for people to settle in and define their space. Back East, Helen Keller explored her socialistic beliefs. The senate and Theodore Roosevelt pursued the Panama Canal project. Immigrants arrived in droves. The NAACP was formed. The Titanic buried hundreds of passengers at the bottom of the sea while the Wright brothers soared to the heavens at Kitty Hawk, South Carolina. Out West, Edwin S. Porter released his technological miracle film, *The Great Train Robbery*, and his new techniques turned the novelty of moving pictures into a wildly popular artistic medium. Big Bill Haywood founded the first major union, the Industrial Workers of the World in the Colorado mining camps. Violence simmered and boiled over in the struggle to establish labor rights. In the Heartland, Henry Ford gave America the Model T in 1908, setting the future in motion. Upton Sinclair published *The Jungle*, exposing dangerous practices in the meat processing industry. Chicago's stockyards were his target—a locale that played heavily in the McHenry County economy. There were joys and tragedies here too, but this patch of river valley home was mostly sheltered. Residents worked hard, went to bed tired at night and had less access to breaking news than we have now. Of course they were concerned about the bigger picture, but McHenry County was busy growing a lifestyle.

MAIN STREET, RINGWOOD—TOWNS WERE MATURING. Ringwood, north of McHenry along Route 31, was a commercial center for people as far away as Rockford. Two Vermont doctors settled it. Soon, merchants moved in. At one point, Ringwood had the largest mercantile store in the area, one of the largest grocers (with a mobile grocery service), a feed mill, smithy, and garage. (Courtesy the Henry and Margaret Szlachta Collection.)

NATIVE AMERICANS. John Waudrack, pictured here, was not a Native American, but he knew about Paleo Indians living here as early as 12,000 BC. Older residents remember their parents telling of looking out school windows to see Winnebago, Ottawa, Chippewa, Pottawatomie, Fox, or Sauk people traveling across the area. Arrowheads are still found today in construction projects. There are at least 10 Native American burial and effigy mounds in the county. (Courtesy the McHenry County Historical Society.)

CHILLING CHICAGO, C. 1901. One of three icehouses owned by Knickerbocker Ice and Consumer Ice. Workers cut from the 10–12 inch-thick covering on Crystal Lake. The task took 6 weeks, employing 250 men. These buildings stored 96,000 pounds of ice for shipment to Chicago during the summer. Some was used to cool theaters—fans blew across huge bins of ice in the balconies. (Courtesy the McHenry County Historical Society.)

OLIVER SHIPPING DEPARTMENT, C. 1907. Foreman Earl Young's crew shipped some 60,000 typewriters at a top rate of 325 per day. The Oliver's advertising claim was the ability to "obviate mistakes" because the type was always in sight, according to the company's ad in a 1903 *Atlantic Monthly* magazine. The people of Woodstock funded the first official Oliver factory in appreciation for its value to the community. (Courtesy the McHenry County Historical Society.)

OLIVER TYPEWRITER COMPANY PUNCH PRESS DEPARTMENT, MERRITT THOMAS, FOREMAN. Unusual for factory settings at the turn of the last century, this one had large windows to flood the room with daylight. Men, women, and children worked side-by-side—imagine the overwhelming daily noise, hot summer days, and winter chill these workers endured for about a dollar a week. (Courtesy the McHenry County Historical Society.)

DOLE AVENUE, SOUTH TOWARD CRYSTAL LAKE. This is one of Crystal Lake's main north-south thoroughfares when it was just a railroad spur serving icehouses. Trains on this spur also brought Charles Dole's guests to his front door at the height of Victorian social life. The City of Crystal Lake bought this land from Chicago and Northwestern Railroad in the 1940s for $16,000 and extended Dole Avenue to the lake. (Courtesy the McHenry County Historical Society.)

C. & N. W. Depot, Hebron, Ill.   3-hir

C&NW DEPOT, HEBRON C. 1900. Traveling meant a train trip. A trip to Twin Lakes, WI, by car meant at least two flat tires along the way. A Hebron history relates: Mr. Pinney built an auto by mounting a gasoline engine to a buggy and gearing it to the rear wheels with a chain drive. How pleased his neighbors were to hear him drive off each morning. (Courtesy the Henry and Margaret Szlachta Collection.)

COUNTY FAIR, 1907. George W. Ferris, Pennsylvania bridge builder, created the Ferris Wheel, engineering highlight of the Columbian Exposition—Chicago's answer to the Eiffel Tower. The original was 250 feet in diameter, 825 feet in circumference. Powered by two 1,000 horsepower engines, its 36 wooden cars each held 60 people. This smaller version certainly garnered as much enthusiasm at the county fair. (Courtesy the Henry and Margaret Szlachta Collection.)

JUDGING AT THE FAIR, C. 1900. This rare image captures the Fair when it was young. Spectators are rapt as judges inspect prize bovines. Animal rumblings could be felt in the pit of your stomach. Dust settled in eyes, hats, pockets, and clothes. Since most people had only two sets of clothes, for work and for dress up, most wore their Sunday best to the Fair and had cause to regret it. (Courtesy the Henry and Margaret Szlachta Collection.)

SCHUETT BUICK DEALER, C.1900-1912. Schuett, a farm implement dealer located off the Woodstock Square where the movie house is now, added automobiles to his line of merchandise. Here, satisfied customers show off their horseless carriages. The *Republican* newspaper, shown right, competed with the *Democrat* and the *Sentinel*. (Courtesy the James Keefe collection.)

ALGONQUIN HILL CLIMB, AUGUST 5, 1909. Not surprisingly, as motorcars grew popular and affordable, drivers developed a need for speed. Races were common, and every year in Algonquin, behind the old post office, motorists raced up the hill road for a prize. They came from three states to compete on Phillips Hill off Route 31. (Courtesy the James Keefe collection.)

FLYING IN THEIR FLIVER. Automobiles were not common in 1905 in McHenry County, but their popularity was growing. Here are Mr. and Mrs. F. Jackman and Mr. and Mrs. E.R. Murphy. Both couples were part of the generation that went from horse and buggy transportation to jet aircraft technology within their lifetime. These folks saw more changes than possibly any other generation has experienced. (Courtesy the McHenry County Historical Society.)

BREWERY BURNS, 1902. A horse drawn fire wagon responded to the Woodstock Brewing Company (Arnold, Zimmer, & Co.) at Mary Anne and Washington Streets. It burned to the ground, May 5, 1902. Owner Emil Arnold never had funds to rebuild his 800 barrel-a-month brewery. He had decided not to renew his fire insurance. This was the eighth major fire at Woodstock Square since the fire department's creation in 1872–1873. (Courtesy the McHenry County Historical Society.)

DACY BLOCK.

DACY IS THE LEADER.

In the Agricultural Implement and Carriage Trade T. J. Dacy is the acknowledged Leader, not only in Woodstock, but for McHenry county. He holds this enviable position because of:

1st, Inherent Ability. Some men are born to govern, some to preach, some to buy and sell. Of the last named is Mr. Dacy. He has a natural aptitude for trade, cultivated and strengthened by twenty-seven years' experience in his one particular line at his present location.

2nd, Fair Dealing. Truthful representations go further than cut prices in establishing a permanent trade. In this respect Mr. Dacy's patrons have learned that if he sold them a plow warranted to scour, it never clogged in the furrow; if a carriage with full leather top, it never turned out to be oil-cloth. Large sales and small profits, and every article warranted as represented, has ever been Mr. Dacy's motto.

3rd, Indomitable Courage. Jealous competitors having tried in vain to down Mr. Dacy, fire in turn attempted to annihilate his business. In one brief hour on March 6, 1880, his buildings and entire stock went up in smoke, entailing a loss of over $18,000. Far from being disheartened, before the embers cooled he had placed an order for 300 buggies—the largest ever given by a retail dealer in Illinois—and other goods in proportion, storing them on the Fair grounds and in barns around town.

4th, Location and Facilities. Mr. Dacy buys in large quantities for spot cash, at special rates, and is therefore able to discount the prices of every competitor. He has over 9,000 square feet of floor space, and his warehouse is provided with a sidetrack, so that goods can be unloaded direct from the cars. This feature is of especial value, both to himself and any possible successor, for a man can not stay always in business. And the writer will venture the assertion that that same possible successor will find the unblemished record made by Mr. Dacy in his nearly thirty years of business of even more value than stock or location.

For anything in Mr. Dacy's line, from a steam threshing outfit to a wheelbarrow, call on him at the northeast corner of the public square, or on any business proposition address him simply T. J. Dacy, Woodstock, Ills.

AD COPY BEFORE MASS MEDIA, c. 1900. Advertising picture cards were still promoting business before radio, television, and national newspapers put mass marketing in the reach of the small businessman. Some cards were simple, like this one, extolling the virtues of Dacy's Agricultural implements, which would become Dacy's Appliances. (Courtesy the James Keefe collection.)

ANOTHER DEVASTATING FIRE, OCTOBER 1907. Marengo Stove Factory, also known as Collins and Burgie Stove Factory, burned in 1907, October 5. It stood north of a site that would be known as "hobo jungle" in the decade following. The jungle of weeds that grew over the ruins was a hangout and overnight shelter for tramps. Nice girls were cautioned never to walk out in that direction. (Courtesy the Henry and Margaret Szlachta Collection.)

RELIEF SIGNED BY KARL SCHNEIDER. From Pittsburgh to Denver, during the time of Art Deco style buildings, orders poured in for American Terra Cotta Industries to create artistic facades for theaters, office buildings, churches, and department stores. The clay was shipped to Crystal Lake at a total cost of $1 per ton. The company also specialized in Teco pottery. Early pieces now sell for thousands of dollars. (Courtesy the McHenry County Historical Society.)

MARENGO OPERA HOUSE INTERIOR. Today, the building survives as a bank. But gone is the elegance of gaslight chandeliers, satin and brocade draperies, and plush seats that cradled the posteriors of farmers, statesmen, suffragettes, and working people as they attended plays, lectures, meetings, and musicals. Everything that comes out of Hollywood in the 21st century has homely roots in the American theater circuit. (Courtesy the McHenry County Historical Society.)

REVEREND **W.A.** SUNDAY. Billy Sunday was infamous all over northern Illinois for his fight against demon rum. A baseball player and evangelist, he traveled everywhere he could to bring the good word to the people. Look at his eyes: Billy was a mesmerizing speaker. Local folk said, "After Rev. Billy's visit to Marengo, things seemed to jell in the community. Bickering and gossip was less noticeable." (Courtesy the McHenry County Historical Society.)

TENT REVIVAL TONIGHT IN MARENGO. Before there were churches, preachers would advertise tent revival meetings and open-air services. Zealous evangelists, like Billy Sunday, drew 400–500 people on summer evenings. Hours of preaching and demonstrating against "wealthy arrogance" usually netted more than $1,000 for the preacher. Hymns were sung, from raucous to soothing—some congregations shouted "Hallelujah" while others quietly affirmed, "Amen." (Courtesy the McHenry County Historical Society.)

OLD CREEK SCHOOL, C. 1906. In Burton Township, this land was dedicated for schools in 1850. The original school burned in 1882 and was rebuilt. This township had the last operating one-room school, English Prairie, till 1961. Dr. Fillmore Bennet, an early official, wrote the ever-popular, "In the Sweet By and By" and other sacred songs. Schools relied on hymns, Shakespeare, the Bible, and McGuffy's Reader because textbooks were scarce. (Courtesy the McHenry County Historical Society.)

UNION SCHOOL, CRYSTAL LAKE. This stately building was demolished in the 1940s. Built in 1883, it schooled Crystal Lake and Nunda children from 1st grade through 11th grade. The building, near the corner of McHenry Avenue and Paddock St., became an elementary school at the turn of the century when the first high school was built. John Husmann Elementary now stands on this site, with Crystal Lake Central High to the southeast. (Courtesy the McHenry County Historical Society.)

SMITH–THROOP GENERAL STORE, NUNDA, 1900. Thriving businesses, like Chicago's Marshall Field's, recognized the value of expanding their markets into outlying areas. They hired traveling salesmen—cultural icons. More than any other marketing advance until E-commerce, the department store and its sales force changed the way America shopped. Pictured, from the left are: Mr. Matthews (traveling salesman—Carson Pirie Scott), Frank Smith, Frank Blaksley, unknown. (Courtesy the McHenry County Historical Society.)

BUSINESS INTERIOR, C. 1900. It's unusual to find interior photos from this era—large windows to let in light were not typical. This is Marengo Bank. Note the extensive use of polished woods that may well have been cut and milled locally. This teller office, austere but functional, was high-tech and considered secure for the time period. (Courtesy Marengo Public Library.)

THE HARVARD GROCERY STORE, C. 1900. Warren Webster makes his purchase from Herbert Megan (in shirt sleeves) as other customers watch the photographer work his magic. Wandering photographers recorded everything they saw in their travels. These little stores were social centers in rural areas. They were usually scrupulously clean, stocked with barrels, boxes, and cans. (Courtesy the McHenry County Historical Society.)

DAIRY INDUSTRY PROVIDED JOBS. If you didn't work on a farm, maybe you worked in the dairies to support your family. In 1900, working conditions were rough—wages non-negotiable. This is Bowman Dairy where Oak Industries would later stand. Front row, from left: Albert Rower, Herman Rower, Henry Dunker, Fred or Willie Bozer. Center: (?) Handrock, Frank Washo, unknown, Bill Rower, unknown. Back: Bill Wilson, Bill Kimball. (Courtesy the McHenry County Historical Society.)

WINTER PLEASURES IN 1909. This post card shows a toboggan slide at the Todd Seminary for Boys. One of their graduates was Orson Wells. Norman Peterson sent this card to his cousin Nell Hill at Yerkes Observatory in Lake Geneva, Wisconsin, where she worked for Professor Frost. Norman said, "This is our slide, don't it look pretty nice?" (Courtesy the Henry and Margaret Szlachta Collection.)

AFTER THE RACE—PISTAKEE YACHT CLUB, C. 1908. The atmosphere at Pistakee Lake was nothing less than highbrow. Wealthy members of the Chicago Republican Party—publishers, senators, and Mayor Big Bill Thompson, built elaborate homes. Their larger-than-lifestyles were filled with yachts, fur coats, hydroplanes, swagger clothes, spats, and back slapping crowds at lawn parties for movers and shakers. Their money financed many entrepreneurial experiments. (Courtesy the McHenry County Historical Society.)

HAVING A LOVELY TIME ... Note the uncomfortable bathing costumes that don't appear to dampen the crowd's enthusiasm as they cavort for the camera. The hedonistic colony of Pistakee Lake homes is visible in the background. After a dip in the lake, these bathers would put on silks and satins to attend neighborhood barbeques, tended by maids and spread with sumptuous food. (Courtesy the McHenry County Historical Society.)

CONSPICUOUS CONSUMPTION—OSTENTATIOUS SETTINGS. Trophies from Pistakee Yacht Club. Political deals were made and broken in this era of excess. Imagine gangsters mingling with powerful men and flashy women. Charles Yerkes, accused of buying votes in more than one election, was part of it. He was cajoled into financing the Yerkes Observatory project, Lake Geneva, at the turn of the century. (Courtesy the McHenry County Historical Society.)

MCHENRY DAM AND LOCKS. The dam was built to create recreational waters along the Chain of Lakes. It was constructed of wood, then steel, then brick, before it was rebuilt by the State of Illinois from reinforced concrete in the late 1930s. Fishermen have cast lines from the dam nearly every day since it was first built. It's a favorite for hiking, boating, and family play time. (Courtesy the McHenry County Historical Society.)

No. 712. TODD SEMINARY SCHOOL BUILDING, WOODSTOCK, ILL.

TODD SCHOOL IN 1910. Prestigious private academies were part of life until the mid 1950s. Lawrence Academy, Marengo Collegiate Institute, Nunda College, and the Todd Seminary for Boys, pictured here, provided quality educational programs. The Todd School, which closed in 1954 after 106 years of operation, was alma mater to Orson Wells, who returned in the 1930s to organize a Shakespearean Woodstock Festival. (Courtesy the Henry and Margaret Szlachta Collection.)

Three

FROM 1910 TO 1919

The 20th century was a decade old and technology came on with a vengeance. There were more cars. Goods could be shipped faster. Industry, even in McHenry County, looked for better, more scientific ways to create, produce, sell, and deliver. Credit was born. Businesses weren't as concerned as they could be about employees. Then a horrendously tragic fire consumed 500 people at the Triangle Shirtwaist Factory in New York and labor reform was a priority everywhere. Entrepreneurs and inventors in McHenry County worked on the same problems that plagued the rest of the nation, while everyone faced one of the most frightening decades in history. A major flu epidemic and the first war that would be called "World War." Think about facing, for the first time, the idea that the entire world is at loggerheads. It was war of machines, a war you couldn't see, you could only hear about it, read about it, and feed your sons to it. Hope was the order of the day here. Women campaigned for social change and reform. Families found more leisure time—pursuing healthy, inexpensive pastimes. While W.C. Handy penned "The St. Louis Blues," local songsters wrote tunes like "In the Shade of the Old Apple Tree." Charlie Chaplain and Mary Pickford were all the rage as people sought ways to forget the mess the world was in.

LAYING BRICKS ON WOODSTOCK SQUARE. Visitors to the Woodstock Square love the quaint paving bricks that cover the roadway all the way around the park. Those bricks were painstakingly laid by hand in the summer of 1912. A bed of sand and pea gravel was put down, then crews installed the brick that has lasted nearly 100 years. This photo faces east, where Lloyd's Paint and Paper is now. (Courtesy the James Keefe collection.)

TERRA COTTA INDUSTRIES, 1919. Walter Heidel, one sculptor for the company, posing next to one of his projects, the façade for a theater in Indianapolis. Once the clay arrived at the factory, employees added water, and kneaded the mixture with their bare feet. American Terra Cotta made Teco pottery lawn ornaments, huge urns, hearths, and columns. This was a time of building, designing, and creating in every town. (Courtesy the McHenry County Historical Society.)

COMPLIMENTS OF COMMANDER STILL. This photograph was autographed to Christiana McBroom by the Commander on May 30, 1911 with his compliments. No prairie town was complete without its war memorial, and the people of McHenry County, according to the inscription on the piece, constructed Woodstock's on March 23, 1909. Woodstock is the County Seat, though originally, McHenry village was. (Courtesy the McHenry County Historical Society.)

44

CANONS ON THE GREEN. Note the gazebo, it is the original built on the Woodstock Square, around the time the soldiers' monument was put up. Two Naval canons (behind and left of the ladies) were removed and melted for bullets in 1942 during World War II. The poster is typical: a Charlie Chaplin movie was opening at the Princess down the street. (Courtesy the James Keefe collection.)

ALL WORK AND NO PLAY—NOT IN MCHENRY. Once, Peter Worts bet $5 he could shoulder a half-barrel of beer and walk from west to east across the bridge near Bickler House. He won. This is Bickler House in 1913. Peter is on the truck, his sister Clara is in the rear of the car with her husband, Ted Bickler. The first McHenry County courthouse was on this site. (Courtesy the McHenry County Historical Society.)

AUTO RACE—WALK UP AVENUE. This may look like a traffic jam, but it's the annual auto race on Walkup Avenue. The street is named for one of the first families to settle in the Nunda area. Cheering spectators lined the street to watch this race—the autos reached incredible speeds of up to 30 mph. Transportation was becoming very important to the county. (Courtesy the McHenry County Historical Society.)

WOODSTOCK AND SYCAMORE TRACTION COMPANY. An ambitious undertaking, this railroad was forerunner to mass transit systems, but it was short lived. The gasoline motorcars ran through Sycamore, Genoa, and Marengo and plans were made to lay track to Wilson Corners in the north. The grading was done but the rights of way were never purchased. Its hey day was 1910–1911. (Courtesy the McHenry County Historical Society.)

CHICAGO & NORTHWESTERN DEPOT, CARY, 1913. Clarence Davis is fourth from left, Lyle Woodbury is second from the right, and Theodore Davis has the stop sign. Railroads expanded at such a heated pace that the C&NW line and the Fox River Valley line got in a feud about rights-of-way. Dozens of tracks, including an electric passenger service that stopped at every crossroad and farm, crisscrossed the area. Abandoned tracks are still in evidence. (Courtesy the McHenry County Historical Society.)

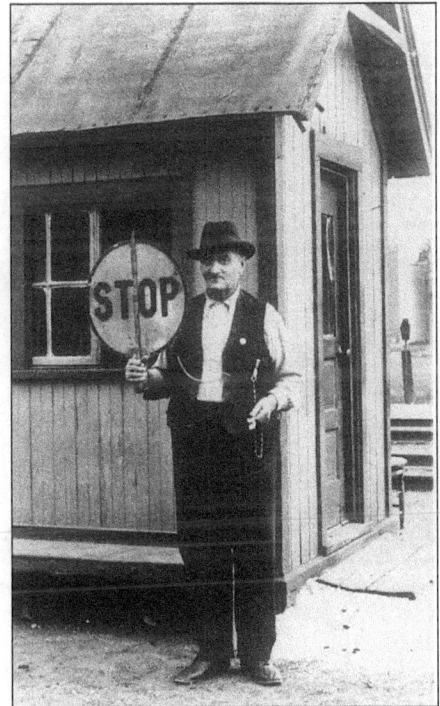

THE CROSSING GUARD. Mr. Schroeder was a railroad crossing guard around 1915 (his granddaughter Elsie Range and his son C.J.C. Schroeder were also county residents). Nearly all crossings were grade level and those annoying automobile drivers ignored mechanical signals. With as many as 47 trains passing through towns daily, the crossing guard was indispensable. (Courtesy the McHenry County Historical Society.)

47

TRAIN WRECK AT CRYSTAL LAKE, SEPTEMBER 11, 1911. In this awful wreck, Hiram Haligus (namesake of Haligus Road near Routes 47 and 176), Virginia Knutson's father, was nearly killed—he was driving the engine that was struck. The brakeman was held responsible on a foggy morning—he didn't see the switch indicator. There were no passengers aboard. (Courtesy the McHenry County Historical Society.)

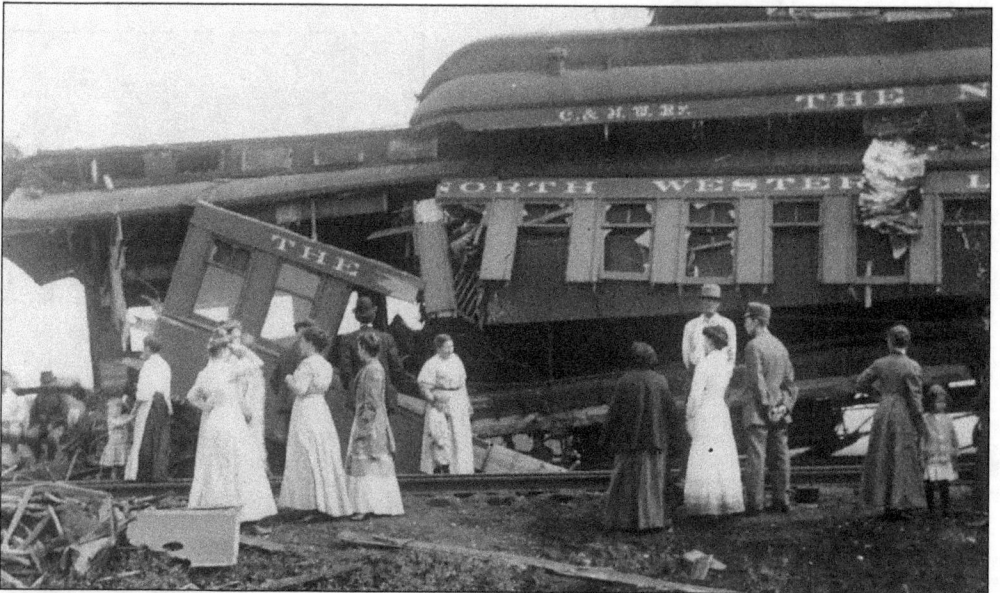

CARS CRUSHED LIKE TOY TRAINS. People came from miles around to look through the wreckage and take pictures with box cameras. Mrs. Martha Sprouse, Sr. and Edythe Leach are among the spectators. It took days for crews to clean up the aftermath of the crash. The image you're looking at came from a family album donated to the County Museum. (Courtesy the McHenry County Historical Society.)

DOWNTOWN SATURDAY NIGHT. Helen Lindow remembers going to town early to get a parking space. Some people drove downtown in the early afternoon, claimed a parking spot, walked home to do chores and returned later dressed up and ready to play. "You could see your neighbors go by as they walked all through the downtown and count how many times they walked by, " she said. It was farmers' night out. Movies were a nickel; each child got a penny spending money. In this picture a horse and buggy, the trolley, and an auto vie for space on State St. (Courtesy Marengo Public Library.)

Fox River Grove Train Wreck. Trains crisscrossed this county from almost the beginning of its history, linking farmers, ice harvesters, and manufacturers to Chicago, Rockford, Milwaukee, and St. Paul. In fact, trains gave the area a reason to grow and build. But wrecks were not unusual—equipment got old, tracks wore away, and people made mistakes. This was a wreck on the Chicago, Milwaukee, and St. Paul line, November 8, 1912. Note the round barn in the background, just right of center—it burned down in 1931 and reportedly belonged to the Opatrny family. (Courtesy the McHenry County Historical Society.)

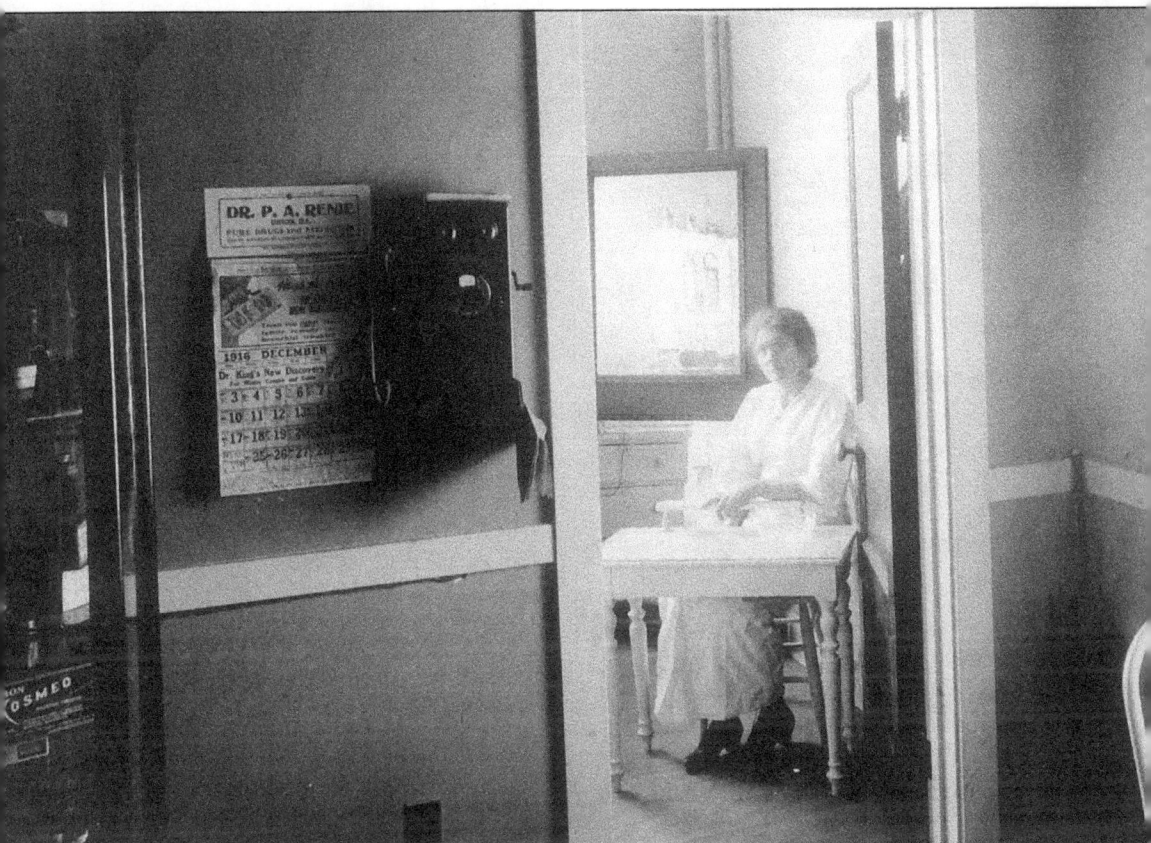

BATTLE WITH A KILLER. The wall calendar shows December 1916. Over the following 18 months this medic, possibly Dr. Ruth Vail Snow, faced the trauma of world war and the tragedy of history's largest influenza epidemic. The quiet farm communities did not escape the ravages of either. Dates and inscriptions in cemeteries tell the sad tale of not enough hospital space, poor quality medicine, and inadequate health care. To add to the gloomy character of this decade, working people like Dr. Snow paid up to 77 percent of individual income to the IRS by the end of the war. (Courtesy the McHenry County Historical Society.)

HOME ON LEAVE. Eugene Shaw, home on leave from World War I. The U.S. Army uniform was a common site and patriotic spirit ran high. This, the first war under the selective service act, required the county to register a quota of 150 men. More than 3,000 actually registered, about half that number served, and 57 perished. The 33,164 county citizens bought $5 million in Liberty bonds. (Courtesy the McHenry County Historical Society.)

TELEGRAM FROM THE RED CROSS. Mothers and fathers trembled when the "tellygraph" delivery person rang the front doorbell. Through two World Wars, Americans would learn of personal tragedies through these tissue-thin yellow missives. This one, however, brought a sigh of relief to Mrs. Green—her son was in the hospital, but doing nicely. (Courtesy the McHenry County Historical Society.)

AMERICAN RED CROSS—OFFICIAL TELEGRAM

WASHINGTON, D. C.

CONFIRMATION COPY

January 8th 1919

CLASS OF SERVICE DESIRED
Fast Day Message
Day Letter
Night Message
Night Letter
Patrons should mark an X opposite the class of service desired; OTHERWISE THE TELEGRAM WILL BE TRANSMITTED AS A FAST DAY MESSAGE.

The   W U   Telegraph Company

Will please transmit the following message by telegraph and promptly deliver the same to the party addressed, for and on account of the American Red Cross.

MRS FRANK GREEN
WOODSTOCK ILL

HAVE BEEN REQUESTED TO FORWARD YOU FOLLOWING MESSAGE FROM PARIS SONS
COMPANY G O.K. MEN IN HOSPITAL BUT IS DOING NICELY TO BEST OF

MY KNOWLEDGE LETTER FOLLOWS SIGNED EDINGER

RED CROSS

W R CASTLE JR

COLLECT
WSI EF

JUNE 10, 1919. The event is the first memorial for casualties of World War I. Pastor Father Conway officiated at St. Mary's Church in Woodstock. Thousands of people passed under the archway that heralded "Our Departed Heroes." Mourners stood in the sun, teary eyed, as flags and bunting rippled in the breeze, bugles blared somber notes, and speakers gave stirring eulogies. (Courtesy the McHenry County Historical Society.)

THE ODDFELLOWS PARADE, 1919. Another celebration in honor of returning World War I soldiers. There wasn't an empty spot at the curb when thousands gathered for the event that was echoed in villages all over the county. The Oddfellows is one of the world's oldest fraternal orders, dating back to 15th-century England. (Courtesy the James Keefe Photo Collection.)

53

THE PATRICK HOUSE ON PRAIRIE STREET. Marengo was the second town established in the county and was originally called "Pleasant Grove." Early on, the Patrick family figured prominently in organizing and building Marengo. They opened a cheese factory during the Civil War. This photo shows the family home behind a wonderful chauffeur-driven car whisking ladies off to volunteer work. (Courtesy the McHenry County Historical Society.)

EARLY FARM FAMILY. Many old families have remained in this county for generations. Four generations of the Hughes family farmed in and helped govern McHenry County. Other farming families had similar roles in the community's early organization. Earl C. Hughes is standing on the bench in this 1910 photo. Earl's father is standing with Earl's mother Marie (left). Uncle Carl Hughes, who later helped Earl with the farm, is seated. (Courtesy Hughes Hybrids, Inc.)

THE GREENWOOD TEMPERANCE SOCIETY. Neighbors fought the good fight—every community, even tiny Greenwood, tried to cover "old John Barleycorn's putrid corpse with a mantle of charity," according to *McHenry County, 1832–1968*. From 1917 to the end of Prohibition, the fight included a bombing incident in McHenry, sour mash put into a pig sty in Hartland Township (the pigs were sorely hung over), and run-ins with the likes of gangsters like Dapper Dan McCarthy, Heimie Weiss, and Al Capone's brother, Ralph, who paid a visit to Woodstock. Political battles ran rampant and it was hard to tell who was trying to clean things up and who was trying to profit from the sale of black market liquor. Yes, there were speakeasies and hidden beer parlors in these quiet farm communities, and drive-by shootings are not an invention of modern times. (Courtesy the McHenry County Historical Society.)

MRS. COON'S GYPSY CHORUS. In one of the collection's most evocative images, young locals posed prettily to promote their concert at Marengo's Opera House, 1915. Opera houses grew up in communities along railway lines from Chicago outward. Production companies loaded large "flats" of scenery on railcars, making a circuit to outlying theaters. Some of the theaters survive to the present, like Woodstock's Opera House, but many are gone. (Courtesy the McHenry County Historical Society.)

THE SUFFRAGETTE LADY MINSTRELS. A group of activists headlined Woodstock's Opera House in October 1918, empowering their sisters and supporting one of society's most important rights. McHenry County women, including the Women's Voting Club, were always highly active in social causes. They fought for libraries, sanitation measures, school curriculum advances, and hospital facilities. (Courtesy the McHenry County Historical Society.)

PROSPERITY FUELED EDUCATION. School districts were organized, schools expanded. In 1911, these students were probably the entire senior class at Crystal Lake High School. Pictured, from left to right, are: (front row)Laura Cassidy (Hull), Mamie Huffman (Wilcox), Ruth Levin (Farren), Ruth Pate, Harold Walkup, Otto Wollenburg, Charles Pingry, Dwight Goodwin; (back row) Mamie Purvey (Burleigh), Maude Spencer Whute (Wubbena), Irma Ritt (Ebel), Carrie Irwin, Edith Leach, Harold Lund, Henry Cowlin, Ray Blackman. (Courtesy the McHenry County Historical Society.)

PINGRY HOTEL, C. 1918. Originally a church hall on Grant Street in 1860, this was a Crystal Lake landmark until townhomes replaced it in the 1990s. Charles C. Pingry made it a hotel in 1889. Three generations of Pingrys operated the establishment until 1958. Other owners filled it with antiques and operated it until the 1980s, making it one of the oldest continuously operated businesses. (Courtesy the McHenry County Historical Society.)

A Songwriter Inspired. Local lovelies like these inspired Burt Van Alstyne, who composed "Pretty Baby," "In the Shade of the Old Apple Tree," and "Drifting and Dreaming." After growing up here, he worked with Harry Williams and Gus Kahn. His mother, Emma Van Alstyne Lanning, was "Aunt Em" on a popular WLS radio show. These young ladies probably worked at the Dairyman Bank, where they are posing. (Courtesy Marengo Public Library.)

Destroyed December 3, 1919. Shown here is the eerie aftermath of a fire that destroyed a grade school next to Woodstock Central High School (now the fire department), one block off the square. The spectacular 6 a.m. blaze was followed a week later by a fire at the nearby Methodist Church. Authorities said arson, and rumors abounded that a pyromaniac set these fires and others. (Courtesy the James Keefe collection.)

PISTAKEE LAKE SUMMER, WHERE THE WELL-TO-DO DID IT ALL, C. 1911. Excursion trains whisked Chicagoans from the city's humidity and heat to pastoral communities where pristine lakes were surrounded by summer cottages. But at Pistakee Lake, wealthy business people built expensively lavish showplace mansions. Summer parties and entertainments drew crowds of wealthy politicos from all over Illinois. The station pictured was on the Chicago, Milwaukee, St. Paul, and Pacific line. Most railroads had nicknames in those days and this was no exception—it was called "C'mon Stop Prayin' and Push." That railroad line later became known officially known as the Milwaukee Road, which is its name today. An entire family could travel round-trip from Chicago to Pistakee Lake for $1, to enjoy picnics, dances, and a great variety of recreational activities. (Courtesy the McHenry County Historical Society.)

FROM AN EARLY GLASS NEGATIVE, 1910. Our history book would be dry and dull save for pioneers of the magical technology, photography. It is generally agreed among experts that Samuel F. B. Morse made the first photograph in America—then a flurry of interest brought serious amateur photographers out of the woodwork. Photography has been called the most popular hobby of any day, ordinary people with ordinary cameras make literally millions of photos each year. This print of Cormack School is from a glass negative by Edward Nothnagel with his Kodak 4x5 box camera. McHenry County's history was recorded by dozens of proliferate photographers and local historians had the good sense to preserve thousands of them. Many of these treasures are under the care of the McHenry County Historical Society, giving the public access to priceless glimpses of the past. (Courtesy the McHenry County Historical Society.)

Four

THE ROARING '20S

The 1920s was the decade that spawned peanut butter, Sacco and Vanzetti, Lucky Lindy, the Scopes trial, and IBM. Congress, in its highly questionable wisdom, passed the 18th Amendment, setting the stage for the Volstead Act that provided enforcement of prohibition of the manufacture, transport, and sale of alcoholic beverages in this fine country. Woodrow Wilson had just left the White House. Temperance people were all wound up from successes in the decade past. The Feds were plotting to become national enforcers and it was off to the races in every village and hamlet coast to coast. America, say the historians, became a nation of crooks, thieves, and lawbreakers. It couldn't be helped. People like alcohol. Alcohol was outlawed. The Feds couldn't be everywhere and there were plenty of entrepreneurs tickled silly to profit from what Herbert Hoover called "a noble experiment." The 1920s started to roar. At first, the action was just in the big cities where money flowed and speakeasies were a snap to establish. Al Capone became, unfortunately, the definitive Chicago personality. Big Al and his hoodlums loved nipping out to the boonies, passing through this idyllic valley on their way to Lake Geneva away from that annoying Elliot Ness. So it trickled down and out to the country—McHenry County was a wild and wooly place for a bit until sanity prevailed and most folks went back to living lives of non-desperate quietude.

CHRISTMAS PARTY AT THE PHONE COMPANY. In the 1920s, party lines were in. Pick up your phone, turn a crank, and say "Hello, Ethel? 64, please."—you'd get the theater. The telephone girls celebrated Christmas at the central office on the east side of the square above the old Chamber of Commerce. Pictured here, in the back row, fourth from left, is Florence Cooney Keefe; the second from left is Ethel McGee. (Courtesy the James Keefe collection.)

Chicago and North Western Railway Company

Date July 10th., 1926

Mr. W. J. Towns, Chief Engineer.

It is recommended that authority be requested for the following improvements:

Location McHenry, Illinois. Galena Division

Description Proposed Installation of Sanitary Toilets in Passenger Depot

It is estimated the cost will not exceed $ 2000

The necessity for this improvement is as follows:

Patrons have complained about outside toilet facilities at this point and have requested that modern facilities be installed. Sanitary sewers are now in operation and it is due to this fact that complaintants feel that inside toilets should be provided.

Approved:

_____ _____ Division Engineer.

_____ _____ Superintendent.

_____

TRAVEL WAS DEFINITELY NOT FIRST CLASS. Travelers objected to roughing it at the McHenry train depot as late as 1926 when they grouped together and made a demand—indoor toilets! The stationmaster sent this requisition to C&NW railroad, asking to upgrade the outdoor facilities to indoor, since sewers were in place. The requisition was approved, and from that point, many improvements were made up and down the line. (Courtesy the McHenry County Historical Society.)

A. DAVID ROBINSON JOSLYN. This gregarious lawyer served as State's attorney and was renowned for his role in the Orpet case. Legal practitioners were important in the struggle to create a secure and prosperous community. The Joslyn family practiced here for well over 100 years from 1851. They helped build chapters of organizations like the Masons, Lions, American Legion, and VFW. Politics was heating up now in the county. (Courtesy the McHenry County Historical Society.)

MONSTROUS CELEBRATION. Note the irony of the headline. "Monstrous" could describe the Klan. During the 1920s, they were active in Kane and McHenry counties. Prize money was offered for recruiting new members. Rallies were family oriented—fireworks and ice cream socials. The Klan had national membership of over one million by 1926. By the 1930s, they were numbered only in the tens of thousands. (Courtesy the McHenry County Historical Society.)

MONSTROUS CELEBRATION

Given By Tri-City Klan No. 245

Sat., June 18

—1 mile west of—
CARPENTERSVILLE

Follow the Arrows off Route 22

$1000 FIREWORKS DISPLAY
NATIONAL SPEAKER
REFRESHMENTS
BAND CONCERT 5 O'CLOCK

K-UNO · KNIGHTS OF THE · KU KLUX KLAN · K-DUO

HONOR

This certifies that

the bearer, KL _Hed Trumble_ whose signature appears on the reverse side hereof, has been found loyal and worthy of advancement in the mysteries of ~ ~ ~

Klankraft

and has been passed to K-Duo, or Knights Kamellia, and is entitled to all the rights and privileges thereof. This certificate also entitles the bearer to all the rights and privileges of a Klansman of K-Uno. In witness whereof I have hereunto affixed my signature and the seal of my Klan.

Signed _Hed Trumble_
KLIGRAPP

VOID AFTER _12/31/27_   KNO _19_ Realm _Ill._

KNIGHTS OF THE KKK. An active Klan Chapter, based in Algonquin, tried to establish itself in the 1920s. This identification made the bearer "loyal and worthy of advancement in the mysteries" of the Klan. A sense of community was important to this area, and social service organizations have been around since early pioneer days. But this club was not one that was bragged about or that survived. (Courtesy the McHenry County Historical Society.)

CRYSTAL LAKE COMMUNITY HIGH SCHOOL, 1922. This is one of the first buildings dedicated specifically for use as a high school. It has had a couple of additions in its eight decades, but the main building looks pretty much the same now. In the front yard is a stately brick archway donated by the Class of '22. Crystal Lake Central High School now occupies this building, with about 900 students. Once, two or three high schools served the entire county. Now, each town has at least one, Crystal Lake has three, and McHenry has two. (Courtesy the McHenry County Historical Society.)

Big Value
MEAT OFFERS

Friday and Saturday SPECIALS Oct. 6 and 7

Rib Roast (FANCY QUALITY) **19c Lb.**	**Butter** (WISCONSIN FANCY CREAMERY) **25c Lb.**
Pure Pork Sausage 2 lb. for 25c	**Pot Roast** (CHOICE QUALITY) **12-14c Lb.**
Fresh Ham Roast (BONELESS & ROLLED)	**Fresh Pork Butts** (YOUNG LEAN TENDER) **13c Lb.**
Bacon (LEAN SUGAR CURED) Half or Whole Strip **15c Lb.**	**Pork Roast** (LEAN TENDER) **9c Lb.**
	Picnic Ham **10c Lb.**
Fancy Chuck Roast **16c Lb.**	**Veal Shoulder Roast** (FANCY QUALITY MILK FED) **15c Lb.**

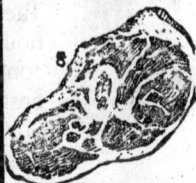

A GROCERY PRICE LIST. These 1920s prices look inviting, but remember, a wage earner made about $50 a month. There was a three-digit phone number at the bottom of the ad—even as late as the '60s, the entire county had one exchange and most people had only to dial four digits. The market was open only until 10 a.m. on Sunday, which gives you an idea of how different life was; few had the luxury of sleeping in. They were up at 5 a.m., at church by 7 a.m., and had marketing done for dinner by 10 a.m. (Courtesy the Henry and Margaret Szlachta Collection.)

ANNOUNCEMENT

John Zenk wishes to announce the **Opening of a Smoke Shop** in the building formerly occupied by Marengo Public Service Co.

A full line of

Soft Drinks, Confections and Tobacco will be carried.

Marengo 6-25-25
ann Book

IF YOU'RE GOING TO DRINK, YOU MAY AS WELL SMOKE. This advertising broadside announces another entrepreneurial endeavor, the smoke shop. In the 1920s, a bit of disposable income helped fuel all kinds of bad habits. The ladies had their hands full trying to keep their men on the straight and narrow, away from rum and tobacco. Some wild women gave up and took up the habits themselves. (Courtesy the McHenry County Historical Society.)

COOKS DRY GOODS, HUNTLEY, c. 1926. Flappers were flapping in big cities during the Roaring '20s, but in McHenry County family life was predictable and organized. On Monday, ladies may have done the wash, on Tuesday, a visit to the village store for household staples, local news, and lively conversation. Cooks' was a family run business from the 1880s. Pictured are Ed Cook and Hazel Lagozaresky, his employee. (Courtesy the McHenry County Historical Society.)

TO MARKET TO MARKET, C. 1920. Not all produce went to Chicago. Local packinghouses dressed meat for residents' use and the corner grocery stores sold fruit and vegetables fresh from the farms. This market was in Marengo—nothing fancy, no neon lights, no electronic terminals. The cha-ching of the cash register was a homey sound as neighbors bought out the locally grown watermelons on this summer day. (Courtesy Marengo Public Library.)

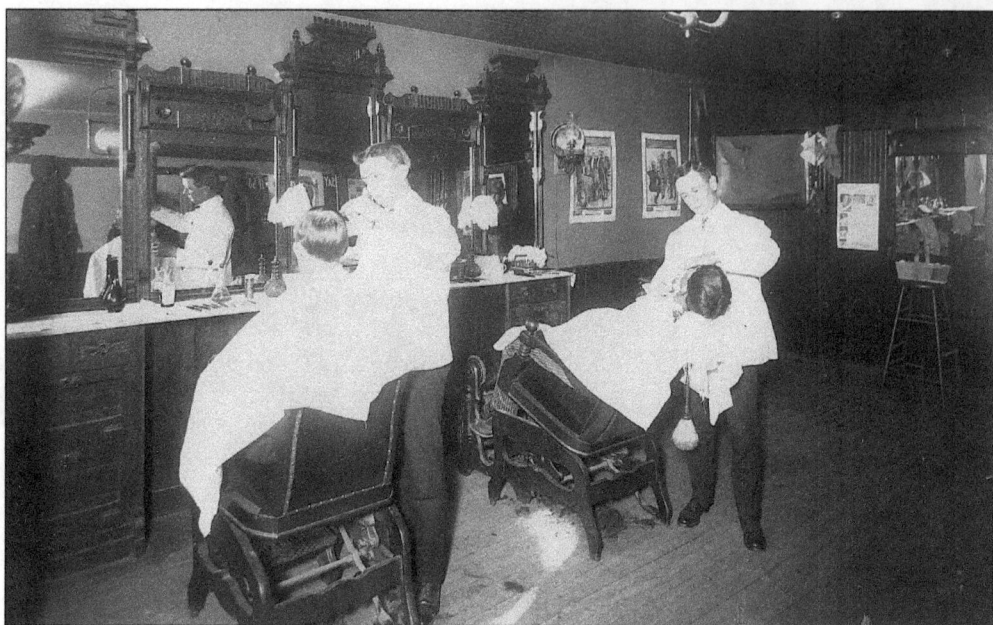

THE SCENT OF BAY RUM AND LAVENDER WATER. Yes, it was a time when frequent bathing was seen as a health risk. But a daily trip to the barber was scheduled for a close shave, a hot towel, and a splash of the manly stuff that gave granddad that clean, nostalgic scent. A shave was about a nickel—the gossip and news shared by barbers and patrons was priceless. (Courtesy Marengo Public Library.)

GLAD RAGS AND GOOD TIMES IN RICHMOND. It's 1926, and theatergoers clamor for the roar of the '20s! At Old Memorial Hall, community members threw off their daytime images and performed an operetta with wild abandon. Pictured, from the left, the third man is Tommy Foster; (back row) the fifth person is Viola Paepke, seventh is Edwin Austin, William Henry Malley, unknown, Edith Vogel, unknown, unknown, and Dorothy Van Every. (Courtesy the McHenry County Historical Society.)

68

OLIVER TYPEWRITER WITH 4-ROW KEYBOARD, C. 1922. One of the "modern" innovations the Oliver crew worked on in Woodstock was the "U" shaped type bars invented by chief engineer Theron L. Knapp. This machine was a prototype from 1922. It was never actually produced, but the "U" shape was used in other production models. (Courtesy the McHenry County Historical Society.)

GARAGES REPLACED SMITH SHOPS, C. 1920. This is Schwalter's garage on Main Street, Crystal Lake. As the 1920s began to roar, automobiles became a fixture in everyday life. Farmers kept their horses, of course, and it's said that seeing a horse tied outside a business was not unheard of right into the 1950s. But autos broke down far more often than horses did—car repair businesses flourished. (Courtesy the McHenry County Historical Society.)

BIGGEST COUNTY FAIR IN THE STATE. What could be more natural in an area that relies heavily on farming to support itself than an agricultural fair to show off the products of the citizens' labors? The fair was first held around 1867, and in various years through its history, was called the largest to be found. The fairgrounds, in Woodstock, encompass 22 acres. This view is 1924, the last fair held before a 25-year hiatus. (Courtesy the McHenry County Historical Society.)

COUNTY FAIR PROGRAM, C. 1920s. A program from the horse race at the fair, complete with notations by the spectator that was following the contests and placing bets. Look closely: each horse's name carries a notation of $5 or $10 bet, pretty hefty sums for the time. The movie ad touts the features at the Princess in Woodstock, admonishing "no matinee—go to the fair!" (Courtesy the McHenry County Historical Society.)

SEATWORK IN STORY FORM. This actual seatwork from a local school, probably in Marengo, shows a progressive attitude. In the 1920s it was still pretty common to find moralistic lessons in all aspects of the curriculum. Allowing children to use nursery rhymes, fiction, and lighthearted reading assignments was modern thinking, and no doubt helped make school attractive to students. (Courtesy the McHenry County Historical Society.)

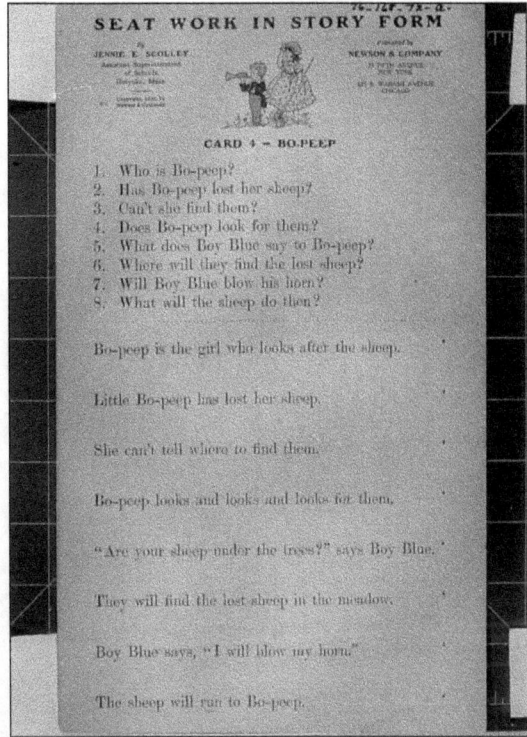

SEAT WORK IN STORY FORM

JENNIE E. SCOLLEY
Assistant Superintendent of Schools, Holyoke, Mass.

NEWSON & COMPANY
15 FIFTH AVENUE, NEW YORK
623 S. WABASH AVENUE, CHICAGO

CARD 4 — BO-PEEP

1. Who is Bo-peep?
2. Has Bo-peep lost her sheep?
3. Can't she find them?
4. Does Bo-peep look for them?
5. What does Boy Blue say to Bo-peep?
6. Where will they find the lost sheep?
7. Will Boy Blue blow his horn?
8. What will the sheep do then?

Bo-peep is the girl who looks after the sheep.

Little Bo-peep has lost her sheep.

She can't tell where to find them.

Bo-peep looks and looks and looks for them.

"Are your sheep under the trees?" says Boy Blue.

They will find the lost sheep in the meadow.

Boy Blue says, "I will blow my horn."

The sheep will run to Bo-peep.

PRAIRIE WINTERS ARE CHARACTER BUILDERS. From earliest days to modern times, winter has been a force to be reckoned with for Midwest prairie towns. Everyone learns to cope as nature hurls blizzard after blizzard across the land. In 1921, with snow piled higher than his head, Ivan Zuelsdorf paused for a photo after claiming this snow fort with an American flag. (Courtesy the McHenry County Historical Society.)

WOODSTOCK TOWN TEAM. From the first traveling team to the championship basketball team in Hebron, sports figured prominently in local history. Pictured, from left to right, are: (bottom row) Tom Bolger, Robert Lounaberg, (?) Sherburne, and H. Huber; (second row) George Swenson, C. Sherburne, Doc Edinger, LeRoy "Pete" Clark, Bill Thompson; (third row) Charlie Zoia, M. Smith, Bill Schoon, unknown, unknown, (?) Dresel, H. Reese, and Fred B(?). (Courtesy the McHenry County Historical Society.)

MOONLIGHT ON CRYSTAL LAKE. The centerpiece of the town nicknamed "a good place to live" since 1922. To that end, an 1884 ordinance closed businesses on Sunday except drugstores, meat markets, and the post office. Cows were banned from grazing in streets. In 1904 autos were restricted to 8 mph. In 1910 a city park was financed, and in 1912 carousel music was mandated to shut off at 9 p.m. (Courtesy the McHenry County Historical Society.)

BATHING AT THE LAKE, C. 1920. The fertile land, which cost about $4 per acre in the mid-19th century, skyrocketed to about $175 in the 1920s. Family fortunes were being made now in business, agriculture, and real estate. Disposable income was not unheard of, recreation costs were nearly nothing, and families headed in droves to the shores of rivers and lakes to play and pose for the ubiquitous family snapshots. (Courtesy the McHenry County Historical Society.)

TRAFFIC BUILDS CAUSING PROBLEMS. Everyone, rich or poor, plain old working people or leisure class, began to acquire autos in the 1920s. Traffic control was an issue, and municipalities purchased electric devices like this, Marengo's first stoplight. This was installed on the corner of Routes 23 and 20. Alas, a careless driver ran it over in 1949. (Courtesy Marengo Public Library.)

LINCOLN MEMORIAL CONNECTION. Karl Schneider, chief modeler for American Terra Cotta, executed these panels for the Lincoln Memorial in Springfield, IL. The company used clay from beneath Indiana and Illinois open pit coal mines to produce decorative sculptures that graced commercial buildings all over the country. The art work's reputation helped put McHenry County on the map. (Courtesy the McHenry County Historical Society.)

HOTEL MAJESTIC BEFORE IT BURNED. Note the decorative terra cotta border on the building and traction motorcar tracks in the street. When the Marengo Fire Department was called to a blaze at the hotel, the department was a few dedicated volunteers. Now, the fire protection district covers a 100-mile area and responds to 300 calls per year. (Courtesy Marengo Public Library.)

Five

THE GREAT DEPRESSION

The Great Depression officially began with the stock market crash on October 29, 1929, but it characterized the 1930s. FDR announced his New Deal, promising a chicken in every pot. McHenry County did its best to produce those chickens, along with eggs, cattle, hogs, dairy products, sheep, seed, food crops, and pickles (the Claussen Pickle company is a McHenry County original). Nationally, John L. Lewis founded the CIO; Vladimir Zworykin, research engineer for Westinghouse, made the iconoscope—the basis of television cameras. Eugene O'Neill won the Nobel Prize for Literature. For the first time, election results were broadcast on the radio. America continued its love affair with cinema, and was dazzled by Technicolor. Shirley Temple, Judy Garland, and all the starlets caused a fashion revolution for those people who could afford to worry about fashions. In the Heartland, tramps and hobos were part of the landscape. People wandering up and down dirt roads desperately seeking work, food, a place to start again. It was typical here to share what you could and hope the world would get back on an even keel. As the 1930s waned, people here were moving to a bright future, improving their schools, expanding their towns, and enjoying what they had.

A DAPPER GENT OF THE 1930s. This is Frank Libuse, son of Thomas A. Czaja, and brother of Mrs. Czaja, both of Algonquin. The photo gives a marvelous feel for the trimmings of country society in the 1930s. The upscale automobile, spiffy double-breasted suit, and gleaming shoes tell you this is a man of substance—life was good, getting better all the time. (Courtesy the McHenry County Historical Society.)

JUDGE SHURTLEFF. The judge said a Capone henchman wanting to corner local beer traffic approached him. Shurtleff said, "He established a place that sold intoxicating liquors with rooms upstairs frequented by women and made the bold assertion that anyone who interfered would be met with a gun." The thug later shot up three McHenry saloons. (Courtesy Marengo Public Library.)

THE THIRD GENERATION. There are more than a dozen centennial farms in the county. Earl C. Hughes started his venture in about 1930. Times were tough—the depression a major factor. Earl recalls people moving up and down the roads with carpetbags, and boiling corn out of farm cribs to stay alive. Pictured, Earl M. tends young hogs. In this decade, fortunes were made and lost on a daily basis. (Courtesy Hughes Hybrids, Inc.)

TRUCK FARM. Though there were corporately owned farms of all sizes in the county during the 1930s, many families relied on "truck farms" like this one for their livelihood. They raised as many vegetable crops as they could and trucked them to the local markets with little or no help from outside the family. The truck farms fed the family and maintained a subsistence income. Often, relatives who had lost everything during the stock market crash moved in with the families who worked the land. This was a decade when people learned a lot about themselves, their neighbors, their nation, and how difficult life could be. Consumer advocates and civil rights laws had their roots in the 1930s. (Courtesy the McHenry County Historical Society.)

ENTREPRENEURS DOWN ON THE FARM, TOO. Surviving the depression required creative thinking. Earl C. Hughes experimented with pollinating varietal oats from state universities. He marketed the resulting seed, creating the Hughes hybrid seed business. Dave Hughes, Earl's grandson, said farmers like the Pelgrens (Pelberry Seed) and Ralph Nichols (Nichols Seed) also produced successful hybrids. (Courtesy Hughes Hybrids, Inc.)

POSTAL STAFF, CRYSTAL LAKE, 1936. Postal delivery brought magazines filled with advertising in the 1930s. Women adopted sophisticated styling that would evolve to padded shoulders and swinging skirts in the 1940s. Men, tired of skimmers and derbies, preferred fedoras. Pictured, from left to right, are: (front row) Walter Southern, Grant McDonald, Arthur Truax, and Tom Church; (center row) Elizabeth Butler, Ed Southern, Laura Reddersdorf, William Harrison, and Alfred Spangard; (back row) Earl Goodwin, Peter Nelson, and William Cowan. (Courtesy the McHenry County Historical Society.)

MAIN BEACH ON A SUMMER EVENING. Though at times the lake has been the subject of arguments about powerboats vs. no powerboats, or who actually owns the lake, it has been a wonderful venue for family activities, moonlight concerts, swimming, and July 4 fireworks. Four generations of people from all over northern Illinois have enjoyed it. Main beach, facing west, is perfect for watching summer sunsets. (Courtesy the McHenry County Historical Society.)

CREATING A RECREATION COMMUNITY, C. 1930. Wonder Lake was once the site of a Pottawatomi village and a settlement called Queen Anne's Prairie. A group of businessmen, called visionaries by some, dammed the Nippersink Creek in 1929. (The engineers involved were also part of the Panama Canal project.) Thousands of residents came by auto, bike, and on foot every weekend to watch the land flood. (Courtesy the McHenry County Historical Society.)

WONDER LAKE, LOOKING TOWARD THE DAMN—THE BEGINNING. Locals collected arrowheads and artifacts from land soon to be deluged. The gates of the dam were closed on February 22, 1930. A trickle began, to the amazement of hundreds of onlookers. Weeks later, the lake was a permanent part of the landscape, and the village that would have, for a time, the largest population in the county was born. (Courtesy the McHenry County Historical Society.)

WONDER LAKE IS BORN—876 ACRES GO UNDER. After the land was flooded, small summer cottages were built and the tiny hamlet developed rapidly with boating, fishing, and swimming, drawing seasonal and year round homeowners. Today, the sound of boats and snowmobiles is part of life in Wonder Lake. The community has no industry and only a small commercial center on the east side of the lake. (Courtesy the McHenry County Historical Society.)

WONDER LAKE OUTLET DAM, 1939. After the land was flooded, the Wonder Lake dam became a favorite fishing spot with clean, sparkling, water and plentiful fish. It wasn't unusual to cook the catch over an open fire before heading home for Sunday evening church services or visits with neighbors. This is a post card—the message on the back is from Verna, writing in glowing phrases of the summer home at Wonder Lake. (Courtesy the McHenry County Historical Society.)

BIRD'S EYE VIEW—VILLAGE OF MCHENRY. This photo was taken from atop the Landmark School, c. 1930s. It shows the Riverside Hotel in the far distance, upper left. The site of city hall is in the lower half of the photo. If you could stand at this vantage point now, you would see nothing but buildings, utility cables, and cellular phone towers. (Courtesy the McHenry County Historical Society.)

EICKSTEADT SCHOOL, C. 1938. Because of hard economic times, some children had to leave school to work; some were able to get their education while juggling responsibilities that would daunt an adult. This is a Riley Township school. What did these youngsters do for amusement in hard times? They may have sat in front of a Philco radio, listening to *Superman*, created in 1938, or *Fibber McGee and Molly*. (Courtesy the McHenry County Historical Society.)

CARY PUBLIC SCHOOL, C. 1935. Mrs. Frank Hubert is the teacher in this very modern classroom, complete with electricity. Note that workbooks replaced slates as times got better, and each student has a textbook, a clear indicator of the district's healthy budget and the community's desire for education and wholesome activities for children. By this time, Boy Scout Troops and 4H Clubs were important too. (Courtesy the McHenry County Historical Society.)

FLATIRON SCHOOL, C. 1931. Mary Buckley was the teacher. Many teachers had only a high school education, but were dedicated to giving children the most and best knowledge possible. School schedules operated around the needs of the farms—children had to do chores and get the crops ready for markets. Teacher salaries ranged between $150 and $200 per month. (Courtesy the McHenry County Historical Society.)

EARLY MAIL CARRIERS. The County gained 2,000 citizens between 1930 and 1940, and developed house-numbering to facilitate "Rural Free Delivery." Pictured here (from left to right) are Ed Southern, Alfred Spangard, and Peter Nelson, sporting official uniforms outside the Williams Street Post Office in Crystal Lake. Elizabeth K. Butler was in her second decade as Post Master; she would serve until 1971, the longest tenure of any postmaster there. (Courtesy the McHenry County Historical Society.)

WOODSTOCK POST OFFICE—1931. This photo was an official record of progress when the post office was rebuilt. The back carries initials from engineers who approved the construction work. The image looks northeast and was taken Dec. 1, 1931. G.A. Geib was the chief engineer; L.A.Simm was superintendent of the building division. (Courtesy the James Keefe collection.)

THE HAZARDS OF AGING BUILDINGS. As the depression approached, money was hard to come by. Buildings in every business district were aging—many were built before the 20th century. Old boilers gave out, wiring that was hurriedly and poorly done overheated and fires were an every day occurrence. Many towns would soon raise taxes and bond referendums to update and expand commercial areas. (Courtesy Marengo Public Library.)

Six

THE '40S AND
WORLD WAR II

Just as the world settled down, the Japanese bombed Pearl Harbor, killing 2,403 Americans. Millions of families, including those in McHenry County, shuddered as the day that would live in infamy played out in their living rooms, on the Philco radio. Citizens sprang into action, volunteering, using ration books, donating anything they could. Everybody planted Victory Gardens. Grandfathers who couldn't ship out joined the Civilian Defense. Farmers stepped up production, using new tools, crop rotation, hired help, and new chemicals. This war was played out under our noses. Newspapers, newsreels, radio broadcasts, war correspondents, and photographers brought it home. During this decade, while a global mentality gave rise to the United Nations and various governments sorted out the war, everyday people's lives leaped into definitively "modern" times. In 1947 a housing development called "Levittown" was built in Hempstead, New York. It was 17,450 homes, built for 75,000 people, in an exact 27-step method with prefabricated material. Suburbia was born. They whipped up as many as 30 new homes daily. Some housing developments grew up in this community, too, and city dwellers looked to the quieter country life, but the second half of the 20th century would be quiet and idealistic for a very short time.

TYPICAL MCHENRY COUNTY FARM, C. 1940. Dairy farms covered the countryside and by the 1920s, major dairies like Bowman and Borden moved in. Horse farms and racing were common too. The result was strong family farms and a booming lifestyle and economy by the 1940s; these farms were a major factor in wartime food production. (Courtesy the McHenry County Historical Society.)

THE WOODSTOCK BORDEN PLANT. Borden arrived in 1902, opening a plant in Hebron that operated until the 1960s. They soon opened installations in Marengo and Woodstock, pictured here, c.1940. In the beginning, milk was taken to market by farmers wearing raccoon or beaver furs, and driving bobsleds. Big dairies put the milk on rails—the C&NW railroad transported a "white river" to Chicago markets. (Courtesy the McHenry County Historical Society.)

WOODSTOCK HIGH MARCHING BAND. For 100 years, the schools here have had a reputation for excellence. Awards and honors were hard won, but not unusual. This is the occasion of one of the earliest—the marching band was invited to the National American Legion Convention in Milwaukee in 1941. So many local people traveled up to see the parade that a radio commentator in Milwaukee said: "They must have locked up the city of Woodstock today, everyone is here!" Clarence Olsen was the band director; a school in Woodstock is named for him. (Courtesy the McHenry County Historical Society.)

EDUCATION IN THE 1940S. It may surprise you to know that children attended one-room schools in the 1940s. Schools were not consolidated until 1947, when McHenry County combined some of their 146 school districts and began erecting larger buildings. Even today, some districts contain only one school. The students in this photo are probably from Fosdick School, around 1940. The teacher was Olive Dugert Hill. (Courtesy the McHenry County Historical Society.)

WOMEN: STRONG AND UNFLAPPABLE. Although worldwide change in women's roles came slowly, McHenry County women were active, capable, and involved in their family's well being from the very beginning. Some went out to work, some helped in the family business. Like other couples, Earl M. and Mildred Hughes shared farming responsibilities. While he was in Washington helping to improve things for those at home, she managed the farm—overseeing herds, laying hens, hogs, corn, and oat production. She kept the business growing, as did many farm wives that were her friends and neighbors. (Courtesy Hughes Hybrids, Inc.)

ON THE EVE OF INFAMY, 1941. Ballroom and swing dancing were as popular here during the '40s as they were in the rest of the country. On the day of this dance, Dec. 6, 1941, county partiers traveled to Milwaukee for good music and a pleasant evening. Immersed in the mellow sounds of the Miller Orchestra, dancers gliding through the smoke filled room, smiling, flirting, would have had no inkling of the tragedy that would play out at Pearl Harbor the very next day. (Courtesy the McHenry County Historical Society.)

WORLD WAR II AND THE BOYS FROM FARM AND FACTORY, C. 1942. Families and loved ones watched draftees board trains to begin military service. Every town had to reassign responsibilities on community boards and in municipal departments to replace departing draftees. Families dealt with rationed meat, gas, rubber, metal products, and other commodities, including food. Farmers worked to supply as much meat and dairy as possible. But by 1945, life became less worrisome as soldiers came home. For example: *The Crystal Lake Herald* reported on Nov. 8, 1945—"Dr. J.C. Scully has been separated from the Navy and resumed his practice as physician and surgeon in Algonquin." (Courtesy the McHenry County Historical Society.)

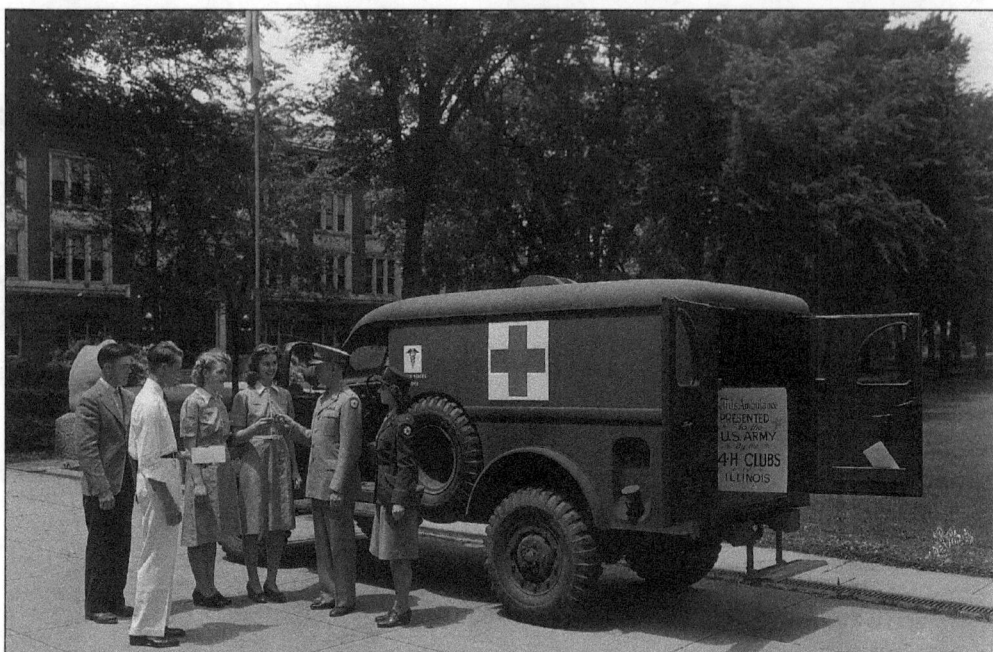

4H Clubs Helping the War Effort. Working to make America safe concerned everyone in the 1940s. Local 4H clubs held fund-raisers, selling their own projects to raise money for the war effort. They purchased an ambulance and donated it to the U.S. Army. The picture was taken in front of Woodstock High School. (Courtesy the James Keefe collection.)

Labor, World War II. Curtis Candy Company, with 4,000 acres of potato and popcorn fields, brought Japanese American workers from California detention camps. The families moved into barracks, pictured here. Newspapers as far away as Propaganda, Alaska, reported the uproar here—city councils debated and parents worried about Asians in the schools. German and Japanese prisoners of war from Rockford's military camp worked here too. (Courtesy the McHenry County Historical Society.)

McHenry Day Parade. In 1947, these ladies marched down Green Street in downtown McHenry as part of another celebration. As community businesses developed, expansion became the byword; Chambers of Commerce put on their thinking caps and brought Sunday afternoon outings a sense of organization and commerce. (Courtesy the McHenry County Historical Society.)

Crop Dusters in the Late 1940s. One of these fellows is Bill Russel, a Township Supervisor and Chairman of the County Board. He was a farmer and had a World War II training plane—crop dusting was controversial, so most often he used his plane for demonstrations like trick landings at the fair or giving barnstorming rides. (Courtesy the James Keefe collection.)

EXPANDING AGRICULTURAL OPPORTUNITIES. Helen Hughes lures her kitten down from stored oats in the barn. Seed oats became a big part of local agriculture. The land was fertile and farmers sought high energy feed for their dairy cattle. McHenry County farmers had a reputation for using their heads and the land to take care of their families while producing food for market. (Courtesy Hughes Hybrids, Inc.)

PROCESSING OATS ON A LOCAL FARM, C.1944. Dean Thomas unloads harvested oats. The truck is dumping the grain into a seed house to await cleaning. Farmers have to be thrifty to survive—parts of this same truck and the seed house itself were in use on the Hughes' farm until 1999. (Courtesy Hughes Hybrids, Inc.)

AN EARLY WONDER LAKE RESIDENT. Sharon Grace Sells Rice was born in Chicago in 1933 and moved with her family to Wonder Lake in 1945. With the lake in the background, Sharon is shown here holding her Sonya Henie doll, which is in the Historic Society Museum collection. She attended Harrison School and McHenry High School. (Courtesy the McHenry County Historical Society.)

THE BEGINNINGS OF MODERN SUBURBIA. After the war, lines between wealthy tycoons and simple farming families blurred. Middle class families moved from Chicago, lured by affordable housing, quiet neighborhoods, and open spaces. This view may be the epitome of non-urban living—cute Cape Cods, mature trees, and wide, paved boulevards. Relocating here meant good schools, friendly neighbors, and lovely churches. (Courtesy the McHenry County Historical Society.)

Aerial View of McHenry's Business District. Looking northeast, this is the intersection of Riverside Drive and Route 120 (Elm Street), a quiet view of one of the busiest sectors of the city of McHenry, *c*.1940. From this vantage point today, you would see heavy traffic on the river. Water skiers, personal watercraft, pontoon boats, and tour boats criss-cross the river like giant water spiders. (Courtesy the McHenry County Historical Society.)

Dignitaries Visit at the Farm. Because of Earl M. Hughes' Department of Agriculture posts under Ezra Taft Benson, the family farm hosted tours and seminars. WGN radio brought guests, and visiting dignitaries came to see how things worked. Here, (from the left) Earl M., Earl Jr., Magnus Frausin of Sweden, and Dean Thompson inspect a grain drill that plants small seed crops like oats, wheat, and barley. (Courtesy Hughes Hybrids, Inc.)

TO MARKET, TO MARKET. From small local cattle yards, livestock was taken to the vast, legendary Chicago stockyards, once the subject of Upton Sinclair's scathing sociological novel, *The Jungle*. The trip was an event—the entire family might go down for a day filled with dust and the potent smell of thousands of animals. It was nearly impossible to hear anything but the din of cattle voices and hoofs beating the ground at one of the largest stockyards in the world. Such a day was the culmination of a year's hard work and meant the farmers could settle up family accounts once more. (Courtesy Hughes Hybrids, Inc.)

THE EDGE OF POST WAR PROSPERITY. These McHenry businessmen, and others like them, would fuel a tremendous growth by the 1970s providing jobs to a burgeoning area. The merchants pictured probably purchased this truck as a donation to their fire department. Pictured, from left to right, are: J. Sheets, Leander Clay, Charles Freund, Chet Stevens, Joe Wagner, Joe Brown, Paul Weber, and Art Oxtoby. (Courtesy the McHenry County Historical Society.)

NEW FIRE EQUIPMENT. The Moose Lodge, established in 1918, donated this respirator to the Woodstock Fire Department in 1949. Volunteer firefighters and Lodge officials posed for the ceremony. Social and business clubs have contributed to the quality of life in McHenry County for well over 100 years, and this donation was a boon to a very busy fire and rescue department. (Courtesy of the McHenry County Historical Society.)

FARMERS GAVE BACK TO THE COMMUNITY. Here, Earl M. Hughes and Earl Jr. are bagging oats in about 1949—note the Hughes' label. The Hughes family was typical in McHenry County. They worked hard and for generations volunteered time to boards and bureaus. Ann Hughes, wife of Earl Jr., served as 63rd District State Representative and held several other public offices. Many of our school boards, county boards, and community boards were originally staffed by farm owners and farm workers who wanted to see their cities and towns develop a strong quality of life. A number of those who presently hold political offices in the county came from farm families. Perhaps that's one reason why McHenry County has more protected open land per capita than any of its neighboring counties. (Courtesy Hughes Hybrids, Inc.)

A WELL-EARNED MOMENT OF REST. Earl M. Hughes is relaxing with the *Journal of Farm Economics*, spring, 1948. This was likely a Sunday afternoon just before dinner. The cultural icons are wonderful: brick and plank shelves, the tabletop radio, and books that were family staples, including *Tom Sawyer*, *The Egg and I*, and *Black Beauty*. Television was finding its way to consumers about this time, but most families hadn't yet made the leap. (Courtesy Hughes Hybrids, Inc.)

Seven

THE AMERICAN DREAM

The Rosenburgs were convicted, Faulkner showed us the South and won a Nobel Prize, Joe McCarthy claimed he personally knew 200 commies, Truman policed Korea, and a national highway system appeared. Dr. Salk gave us the polio vaccine, we coined the term "teenagers" (and the world was NEVER the same), rock and roll was born, and Elvis Presley rattled Ed Sullivan's stage. America embraced television—the one-eyed monster coughed up *Your Show of Shows*, Mary Martin's *Peter Pan*, Red Skelton, *Boston Blackie*, and *Winkie Dink*. Thus came the era when news happened right before our eyes. People grew wary of the Russians and fearful of nuclear attack. Fallout-proof bomb shelters cropped up here and there while children crawled under their school desks and covered their heads in case of a nuke attack. In a few years, we would stand amazed when President John F. Kennedy's life was snuffed out on national broadcast television. On the home front, McHenry County farms grew into big business. Hired help became a necessity. Small truck farms were sold to housing developers and subdivisions sprouted like alien crops. Some farmers turned to new equipment, machines, chemicals, hybrid seed, and prefabricated buildings—while small farms were vanishing, others expanded to thousands of acres. The community built new schools, churches, parks, and infrastructures to accommodate new settlers coming west out of Chicago. Life here seemed calm, peaceful, and as secure as *Father Knows Best*.

HEBRON FOX CLUB, C.1955. Hunting was popular until animals were displaced by progress. Hebron's Helen Schultz remembers the Fox Club and says foxes are returning to McHenry County. Pictured, from left to right, are: Glenn Bottlemy, Henry DeHaas, Harold Kingsley, Sam DeYoung, Ernest Fink, Ervin Bottlemy, and Edward Berry. (Courtesy the McHenry County Historical Society.)

GENESIS OF AN EMPORIUM, MARENGO, C.1995. The dentist is no longer in the window—if this building could tell its own story, you might learn where he went. But the building was the First National Bank from 1871 to 1917, then Swonger Furniture, then an undertaker's business. Next, it was the Marengo Farm Store until 1942; it slipped into an incarnation as a shoe store, then Marie Anne's Dress Shop by the 1950s. (Courtesy Marengo Public Library.)

LOOKING SOUTH AT STATE AND PRAIRIE STREETS, MARENGO. Buildings have been somewhat modernized, since city ordinances define construction code standards. Some old structures have been torn down, and more will be lost in an effort to beautify the downtown areas and create safe, modern business districts. This shot was sometime around 1953 (note the new Buick) and Marengo's face-lift was underway. (Courtesy Marengo Public Library.)

LOOKING SOUTH AT STATE AND PRAIRIE STREETS, MARENGO, C. 1961. Citizens updated and spruced up their towns. Tract housing, aluminum siding, and prefabricated buildings cropped up to replace or augment stately old structures left from days gone by. But the new generation sees value in antiquity. Historic preservation committees form and a deep respect for the past develops. (Courtesy Marengo Public Library.)

CITY PARK, CARY, C. 1950. The young lady standing is "the Marek girl," with Violet Marcks. The church in the background was home to a Lutheran congregation. A shopping center replaced it. The home of the first Europeans in the county was on the outskirts of Cary. The Samuel Gillilans settled in McHenry Territory, named after a Black Hawk War general. Cary is now a thriving industrial center. (Courtesy the McHenry County Historical Society.)

EXPLOITING TOURISM IN MODERN TERMS. Marine Day, organized in 1948 to celebrate summer on the river, became a permanent fixture as McHenry grew. Later, the festival moved off river and into local parks so more people could participate. Every town developed its own festival, and many of those events are still held today, some drawing national attention. Here, noted model Carol Jensen instructs queen contestants on charm and poise. Front row, from the left: Shirley Conway, Joyce Krumwiede, Carol and Marlene Arvidson, Doris Dermott. Pictured, from left to right, are: (center row) Judith DeCicco, Dolores Mercure, Carol Ann Engh, Elaine Vycital, and Shirley Berthoux; (back row) Shirley Thurlwell, Jackie Moss, Judy Fround, and Lois Claybaugh. This photo was taken by Max F. Kolin and is now part of the County Historical Society collection. (Courtesy the McHenry County Historical Society.)

WHIPPLE DRUGS, DOWNTOWN CRYSTAL LAKE. Resembling a 1950s television setting, Whipple's illustrates a lifestyle not far from that ideal. Small businesses had little competition from chain stores. The telephone business office was also at 112 N. Williams St., from May 1929 to January 1956. The recreation center next door provided bowling and billiards. This building later became Crystal Lake Drugs—in business until summer, 2000. (Courtesy the McHenry County Historical Society.)

EARLY COUNTY COURT HOUSE IN WOODSTOCK, C. 1950. Note the autos around the square: a collector's paradise. This postcard, sent to a friend by a vacationer on the way to Lake Geneva, is an image of the courthouse (built in 1847) which served the county until the 1970s. It currently houses a restaurant and the Dick Tracy museum (Tracy's creator Chester Gould was once a Woodstock resident). (Courtesy the James Keefe collection.)

NEW EQUIPMENT AND NEW FEARS. There were air raid warnings on radio, on TV, and in the newspapers as the Cold War escalated. Many communities actually sounded a local alarm every Tuesday at 10:30 a.m. for practice. Families considered storing emergency supplies of food and water in their basements—some actually did it. First National Bank of Chicago built a 140 foot-square "nuke proof" underground vault in McHenry County, and that vault is still lurking in the ground. But farmers were concerned with financing new technology and buying better equipment to improve their yield. This is a grain dryer introduced by the Mathews Company still making farm equipment in Crystal Lake. The dryer reduces moisture content, allowing farmers to consistently carry acceptable yields to the grain markets. (Don Peasley photo used with permission.)

LIFESTYLE, C. 1955. The norm was a home, three kids, and a dog. Mom stayed home. Girls wore skirts, boys—blue jeans. Wind rustled leaves, chickens clucked quietly, and a tractor rumbled in the distance. Doris Day and Mickey Mantle were role models. With the Beatles on the horizon and the sexual revolution looming, by the time these kids finished college, life would be louder, faster, and far less predictable. (Don Peasley photo used with permission.)

REMODELING WOOLWORTH'S BUILDING. "Modernize" was a 1950s ideal, so this building got a face-lift. Five and dime stores are long gone. But you would be hard-pressed to find a baby-boomer who doesn't remember taking a dollar or two to the dime store to Christmas shop for the whole family. Wandering those aisles, touching and wondering at the sheer quantity was more satisfying than shopping on the internet could be. (Courtesy the McHenry County Historical Society.)

FIRE AT DACY APPLIANCES, WOODSTOCK SQUARE, 1957. McHenry County's most prolific photographer, Don Peasley, shot this image. He covered the entire county, documenting events for 50 years and preserving a major part of history. He caught this dramatic battle against yet another fire on the Square. Ironically, Peasley had a major photographic project being finished at the Allied Print Shop behind the appliance store—it was burning as he shot this film. Fire

department historian Phil Parker said the fire began around noon on an autumn Saturday. The blaze was attributed to a faulty old furnace in the appliance store. Both businesses reopened after extensive remodeling and operated for some years. Note the state-of-the-art Maytag wringer washing machines and window air conditioning units on the sidewalk. (Photo by Don Peasley used with permission.)

A WINNER. A young man worked hard for many months to raise a prize winning cow, but hearing the barker at the County Fair call his name as a winner made it all worth while. Here was a time of peace, between the Korean and Vietnam conflicts, when young men could grow up calmly, go to school, and learn skills that would spawn the age of technology. (Don Peasley photo used with permission.)

THE END OF THE WOODSTOCK TYPEWRITER COMPANY. In 1949, the county's last remaining typewriter company, Woodstock Typewriter, sold to R.C. Allen Business Machines. No one knew the typewriter would be obsolete by the end of the 20th century. Here, a class of Woodstock students practice their keyboard skills on Allen typewriters. (Don Peasley photo used with permission.)

110

THE 1950S: MODERN TECHNOLOGY AND DAIRY FARMING. In 1953, this farmer acquired a bulk milk tank that greatly simplified the daily processing of milk. Every innovation meant more time and cost efficiency. In the post-war era, farmers began to see some additional leisure time, but not as much as the rest of America was enjoying. (Don Peasley photo used with permission.)

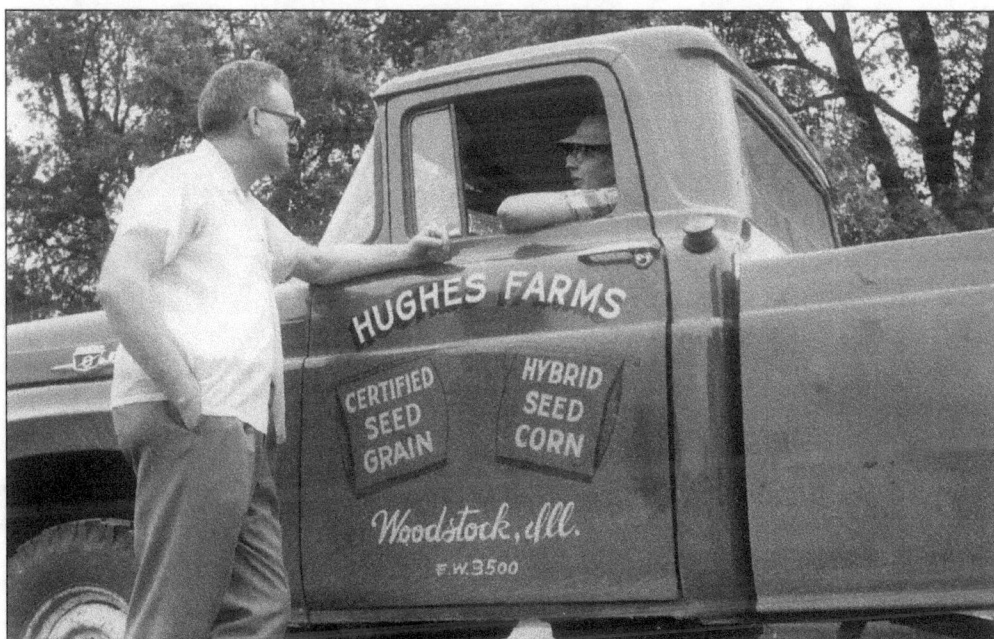

A NATIONAL POINT OF INTEREST. By the 1950s, John Stroham, editor of *National Wildlife Magazine*, was a familiar visitor. He, like the agriculture staff from WGN Radio, became involved in McHenry County because of the close proximity to Chicago. It was Ike's administration—Earl M. Hughes commuted between Washington D.C. and the farm, bringing noteworthiness to the area. (Courtesy Hughes Hybrids, Inc.)

THE SENECA SOCIETY. Convened in 1855 to raise money for George Washington's home, Mt. Vernon, the club may be the county's oldest social group. It became a literary society—one member read aloud while listeners worked on sewing and mending for the hostess. Club rules prohibited gossip or idle chatter. On the 100th anniversary, these members dressed in family heirlooms. (Don Peasley photo used with permission.)

FOUR GENERATIONS OF SENECA LADIES. Anna Pugh, seated, was the oldest member in 1955. Behind her are her daughters Gladys Pugh Perkins and Marguerite Pugh Sherwin. Behind Gladys, her daughter, Marguerite Perkins Lange. The child is M. Lange's daughter Donna Jean. The group met at the Grange Hall on Franklinville Road, now a private home. (Don Peasley photo used with permission.)

SHEEP FARM NORTH OF WOODSTOCK, C. 1953. The 1950s saw the development of new farm chemicals, like anhydrous ammonia, for agricultural use. Farmers had easier access to antibiotics and food supplements for the herds, too. Self-propelled combines, grain dryers, milk tanks, barn cleaners, and silo up-loaders were some of the innovations that contributed to the growth of larger family farms and corporate farms. The average spread went from around 100 acres to over 1,000. Sheep farms were unusual, but they did exist. Crop farms and dairy farms were still more the rule. (Don Peasley photo used with permission.)

VISITING DIGNITARIES, C. 1952. The International Agricultural Economics Group visited McHenry County to learn about the newest technology and methods. In this photo the two men holding their hats are Earl C. Hughes (left) and John Albrich, a neighboring farmer. The tractor and combine are still in use today. (Courtesy Hughes Hybrids, Inc.)

A FARMER WITH HIS TRACTOR. In every era, farmers had to be thrifty. Fathers taught sons to maintain equipment. Often, machines were repaired for decades and then broken into useable components when they gave up the ghost. You'd be hard pressed to date this photo just by looking at the tractor model or the farmers work clothes. (Don Peasley photo used with permission.)

CATTLE FARM IN CENTRAL MCHENRY COUNTY. This family, possibly the Thurlow Yorks, was typical. Though modern chore machinery made it possible to maintain larger herds, cultural changes during the 1950s and 1960s often spelled the end of the small family farm. These children probably did not grow up with a life of working the land. (Don Peasley photo used with permission.)

THE RESULT OF GOOD HARD WORK. This is an example of the corn produced in McHenry County and marketed throughout the world. This is Hughes Hybrid's product, developed for less cob, larger kernels, and uniform seed. Family names like Goebbert, Drendel, Eising, Lilja, Hughes, Bentley, and others have been connected with farms that have operated continuously for as many as 150 years. (Courtesy Hughes Hybrids, Inc.)

McHENRY COUNTY THEATRE GUILD

Presenting

THE WOODSTOCK PLAYERS

NOTABLES AT THE OPERA HOUSE. This autographed playbill from the 1950s gives a surprising catalog of some of the famous actors who performed in rural McHenry County. None were famous at the time, but all were destined to become movers and shakers of American entertainment. Woodstock was to Chicago what off-Broadway was to Broadway—a place to try out new talent or new scripts on a paying audience. Paul Newman, Ann Margret, Tom Bosley,

McHENRY COUNTY presenting THE WOODSTOCK PLAYERS

Opera House Theatre
Woodstock, Illinois

Lois Nettleton, and Geraldine Page were all active in stock productions at the Opera House. Count Leo Tolstoy and Jane Addams had appeared on stage decades earlier to speak about social causes in this building that cost under $25,000 to build and nearly $1 million to restore. (Courtesy the McHenry County Historical Society.)

RESTORING THE OPERA HOUSE PORTICO. In 1997, the Opera House was completed after years of restoration and rebuilding. The final step was to reconstruct the front portico as it was when the theater was built. Original pieces of the wrought iron trim were found and reassembled. The result, according to all involved, was worth the effort. (Courtesy the James Keefe collection.)

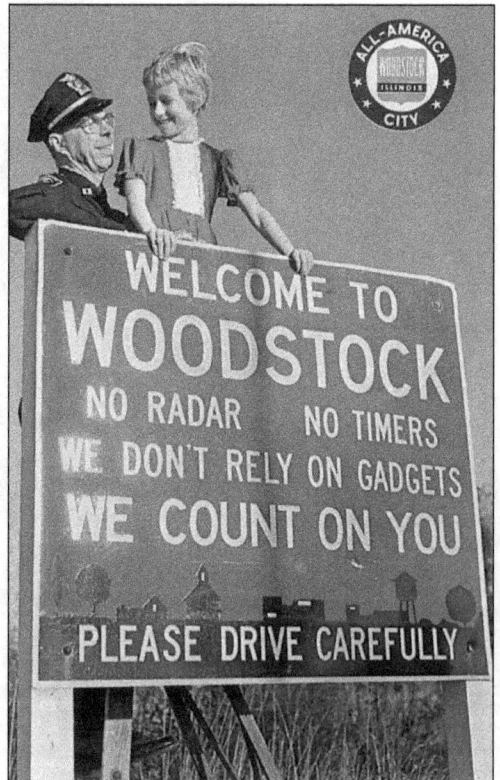

THE HONOR SYSTEM. In this decade, as traffic snarled, communities that had no radar attempted to let motorists' consciences be their guide. It didn't work. Down came the sign, and radar was installed in police cars, according to local historian Jim Keefe, whose collection of county memorabilia began with the purchase of a roll top desk made to accommodate a Woodstock typewriter. The desk's history intrigued Jim—the rest is history. (Courtesy the James Keefe collection.)

WOODSTOCK FIRE DEPARTMENT, C.1999. Buildings are safer as the 20th century winds down—fire companies have better training and equipment, but they owe their evolution to firefighters of the past who learned by trial and error. Firefighter/paramedic Pat Keefe, fourth from the right in the back row, is part of a family that has lived here for four generations. His father James Keefe lent his photos to this book. (Courtesy the James Keefe collection.)

A BEAUTIFUL ALTERNATIVE TO TRACT HOMES. This photo, shot at the turn of the 21st century, shows one reason why some people chose to live away from urban centers. There are certainly modern housing developments in McHenry County, but a short Sunday drive takes you to pastoral settings with cows, sheep, amber waves of grain, and stately homes that have stood the test of time. (Photo by Maryan Pelland.)

THE MORE THINGS CHANGE, THE MORE THEY STAY THE SAME. Businesses and residents keep pace with modern technology and traffic snarls the roadways, but in some quiet corners, it's hard to see that. This photo of Ridgefield's main intersection was taken in November 2000. If it weren't for the automobiles, it could be 1900 in the sleepy little antique town that began as a railroad stop and ended up as a collection of quaint antique stores and art galleries. (Photo by Maryan Pelland.)

DOLE MANSION, DECEMBER 2000. After the market crash of 1929, the house was sold to Franciscan priests as a seminary. Remodeling was haphazard with no intention of preserving or restoring. The house fell into extreme disrepair after standing empty from 1970 to 1977, when First Congregational Church purchased it and renovated the annex as a community activity center. Now, the Dole Mansion Society is restoring the home and it is for sale again. The mansion will survive, as it has for more than a century—echoing the hearty spirit of the communities that surround it. The past is cherished in every town and village; the future is bright and hopeful, and the present is where we live and work to create an excellent quality of life. (Photo by Dan Pelland.)

JULY 4, 1954. Here's the VFW Independence Day extravaganza in Woodstock's Emerickson Park. Crowds were small because of a threat of storms. But the promise of fireworks, the desire to express their patriotism (the war ended less than 10 years before), and a good old family picnic still drew an audience. The gentlemen of the area would have found it hard to pass an opportunity to win that snappy Dodge V8 in the center of the photograph. Note the way folks are dressed: America had still not given up donning their Sunday best for public outings. Ten years later, at the same event, people in the crowds would be more likely to sport jeans, hot pants, mini skirts and granny dresses. (Don Peasley photo used with permission.)

Eight

TURNING THE CENTURY

In the second half of the 20th century, technology swept the world along at a dizzying pace. The moment we grasped and embraced an idea, it was whipped out from under us to be replaced by something new. If you think back on the journey from 1950 to 2000, the mind boggles and you have to wonder how anyone coped with the changes. We traveled to the moon and beyond, endured the sexual revolution, survived the '60s and '70s, put pedal to medal on the information highway, and watched our planet shrink to a global economy. McHenry County communities found a way to deal with the frantic haste and sometimes frightening storm of change. They built, shaped, and polished a group of communities labeled with the epithet, "a good place to live." They carried family values and ideals intact through the maze of progress and modern evolution. They've kept pace with the times and contributed heavily to the betterment of the world. People from this county have made their mark in every aspect of history. But they never lost site of the reasons they came here to begin with.

STICKNEY HOUSE. George and Sylvia Stickney built this in 1856. Sylvia was a spiritualist, not unusual for the time. Her insight was trusted, and her beliefs sincere. The house has no corners and the front door is curved so spirits could float freely in séances. It's on the National Register and may be the second oldest in the area. It's the Bull Valley Village Hall now. (Photo by Dan Pelland.)

RIVERSIDE HOUSE AND STEPHEN A. DOUGLAS. This hotel/rooming house was built in 1864 as a double log cabin on several acres of land. At the time, half the cabin was used as a school and half was a tavern—an odd combination to be sure. Stephen A. Douglas spoke to a crowd here, and legend has it that he converted most of the county into Democrats. Interestingly, his one-time opponent, Abraham Lincoln, had been the first Republican Presidential candidate (dissatisfied Whigs and Democrats who cajoled him into joining them formed that party). In 1916 the cabin was transformed into a hotel with ornately turned wood trim, railings, and balconies. It had a gambling room in the basement and a ballroom on the third floor. The present owners operate the building as a rooming house and hope to restore it. (Photo by Dan Pelland.)

ON LILJA ROAD IN CHEMUNG TOWNSHIP. This large white barn has a roof shingled with ash. It was built in the 1920s and is now a horse barn. At one point, it burned to the ground and was rebuilt on the original foundation. A bank trust, a CPA, and a veterinarian have recently owned the building. (From the County Historical Society's Self-Guided Barn Tour.)

EAST OF ALDEN ROAD. This barn in Hartland Township belonged to the O'Brien family for 100 years. Ed McGovern lost an arm when the barn was blown down by a cyclone in 1903. The very attractive stone foundation is original. Local amateur photographers photographed the four barns in this chapter for a self-guided barn tour during the "Year of the Barn" project in the 1990s. (From the County Historical Society's Self-Guided Barn Tour.)

POST AND BEAM BARN JOINED WITH WOODEN PEGS. Workmen given room and board as part of their pay put this barn together over two years, *c.*1910. On the Hughes farm it was used as a dairy barn until 1985 and is a fine example of an L-shape with Gambrel roof and stone foundation. Gambrel is a double slope roof—the upper slope is less pitched. (From the County Historical Society's Self-Guided Barn Tour.)

RED BARN WITH GAMBREL ROOF, CHEMUNG TOWNSHIP. This is an excellent example of a Gambrel roof. There's a milk house in the center, two concrete silos with domed metal roofs. At one point, possibly around 1936, the barn burned and had to be rebuilt on the original foundation. The barn belonged to the Lilja family for the most part, though it was sold to other farmers once or twice. (From the County Historical Society's Self-Guided Barn Tour.)

126

HOWARD-MASS BARN, LARGEST IN THE COUNTY. This rambler is 350 feet long with 120 stalls. Built in 1942 for industrialist Frank Howard, it housed his American bred saddle horses. Howard, owner of a brass and magnesium foundry, perfected the process for casting nose cones for B26 bombers in 1945. The barn, converted to dairy use before the city took it over, is on McCullom Lake Road. (From the County Historical Society's Self-Guided Barn Tour.)

THE KING SCHOOLHOUSE, KING ROAD, HARTLAND TOWNSHIP. Not everything can be preserved or restored and progress brings change. There are modern farms, factories, and amenities in the area; the contrast between old and new is as apparent throughout the entire county as it is in this image of a one-room schoolhouse that couldn't be saved. But McHenry County has always had an advantage that many communities don't have. Our cities, towns, and villages worked hard to keep pace with progress: there are dynamic opportunities here. It's definitely not a dying area. So younger generations are inclined to stay, or leave for a while and come back to help their hometowns grow, with all the benefits of small town living and all the advantages of 21st century technology. (Photo by Maryan Pelland.)

www.ingramcontent.com/pod-product-compliance
Lightning Source LLC
Chambersburg PA
CBHW050923150426
42812CB00051B/2126